THE MEANING OF LIFE

Mae Louis

BALBOA.
PRESS
A DIVISION OF HAY HOUSE

ISBN: 978-1-4525-5839-4 (sc)
ISBN: 978-1-4525-5840-0 (e)
ISBN: 978-1-4525-5841-7 (hc)

Library of Congress Control Number: 2012916580

Balboa Press books may be ordered through booksellers or by contacting:

Balboa Press
A Division of Hay House
1663 Liberty Drive
Bloomington, IN 47403
www.balboapress.com
1-(877) 407-4847

Printed in the United States of America

Balboa Press rev. date: 11/08/2012

A Message To The Reader

The author of this book does not dispense medical advice. Any suggestions for techniques, treatments, or life-modifying changes should be undertaken with a licensed physician, therapist, or healthcare specialist, and with your own careful analysis. Author's goal and honest intention- to share a spiritual inspirational and awakening revelation. Author and publisher assume no responsibility for individual action or outcome.

To God

****

You are the light and source of my existence. Eternal gratitude from the deepest realm and spectrum of my being.

Contents

INTRODUCTION

The premise of this book is devoted to God. It is only through his divine presence within me, my deep faith and trust in God, which has enabled me to heal myself and become whole again. **I feel compelled to write my story, and share with others, how you can overcome great obstacles in life.** Now more than ever, everywhere you look, there are tortured souls out there. Who are so lost, they cannot tolerate their own existence. To the point of despair, hopelessness, anger, hate, resentment, and disregard for their souls. If I can survived through horrible child abuse, a deprived childhood, and betrayed by the person I love more than anything in this world- my mother, who has ingrained into my being: "I am dumb and stupid, and would not amount to any degree in life," then so can you.

I want to share my love for the world, because my love for God is so great. I am only a humble servant. He has shown his love for me in considerable immeasurable depth. In return, I will dedicate kindness to others, in my most sincerest form of eternal gratitude.

Throughout my life, I have often wondered and asked myself: **"What was the real purpose of my existence?** When life is not kind, it forces you to examine the true depths of your soul. To find answers and meaning to why events happen. That "why" occupied most of my life. The very essence of my existence seems like a blur, or even a dream that I wish would evade. For the longest time, I did not like my being. Reasons that were beyond my control. For instance, there are events in each and everyone's lives, that shape or mold their thinking and behavior. This is why we must find that sense of purpose in ourselves. To decipher the real purpose for our living, before we can fully have a meaningful life. **To me, without the rhyme and reason, I have no purpose.** I started to ask myself: "What does all these life experiences mean?" This search has taken fifty years to unraveled, and to fully understand the true essence of my being.

The main objective is based solely on one subject- a spiritual assessment of the soul. Being raised a Catholic, I understood the teachings were meant to be guidelines, on how we should live our lives. Having an analytical mind, I was not satisfied with what was being taught to me. I had to have rational and concrete answers, which I felt the bible was lacking, and therefore could not provide. My journey has been a lengthy and difficult one. Tragic, for I almost lost my soul. It is through this endeavor, which I have finally found my answers. The pieces to the puzzles have come together, and it all seems to fit.

It is with my good intentions to share this invaluable knowledge to others, **in the search for absolute truth. Reaching out to all those helpless lonely souls, who felt betrayed, hurt, damaged, to remind them I truly empathize with their pain.** I have been through my own hellish depths of despair and back. Please, do not ever give up! There is hope. I am living proof, being a tortured soul myself. I became so sick and tired of being sick, I wanted to changed myself for the better. I did not do this for anyone, but for my soul. Eventually with clarity, I comprehended salvation was the only alternative in life.

I can assure you (just as I have), when you ultimately find your true selves (your own meaning of life), it will effectively modify your destiny, and further resonate down to future generations to come. This is my belief and inspirational purpose in life. **As a small measure, I feel I can make a difference in this world, a means**

to benefit mankind and the human race. In this book, I shall reveal to you my spiritual awakenings. The gifts and powers I have attained, which I now realize were all from God. **I further explain in later chapters, how everyone can obtain these priceless gifts and abilities, where no amount of money can buy.**

Mae Louis

CHAPTER ONE

HEAL THY SELF

Annie: "The sun will come out tomorrow."

We came into this world to be essentially loved, nurtured, and accepted. When this does not happen, the odds are against us. For one becomes lost, with inadequate feelings of despair, anger, resentment, hurt, and emotional pain that will ultimately have dire consequences throughout one's entire life. We become plagued with self-pity, have lack of confidence, low self-esteem and a sense of uncertainty, which dramatically affects our daily existence, and work environment. This perhaps explain why certain individuals tend to compensate their void, or emptiness, and mask their pain with drug addiction.

I made a clear choice early on in life, not to have any toxic dependencies, or follow my parent's poor habits to further complicate my life, as it already has. You can also do this, and be strong for yourself. Everyone possesses free will and control over their own destiny, and do not need anyone to devastate their lives any further. If your role models have certain bad habits, do not imitate their destructive behaviors. All parents are imperfect human beings. Be wise to make that difficult decision whatever it may be, follow your heart and instincts. **Allow the good intellectual side to guide you.** If your social contacts consume large quantities of intoxicants (alcohol, drugs, etc.), you are in most likelihood following the wrong crowd and jeopardizing the healthy mind, spirit, body elements. In order to lead a productive life, it is necessary to associate with others who are heading in the right direction, or leading a wholesome lifestyle. Remember, the dark side is constantly lurking beside, to take control of your soul. The **devil desperately wants your soul, for it is your most prized possession. I cannot emphasize this enough.**

Do you **know why most of us take our souls for granted?** It has taken me a great length of time to realize this myself. The answer: **Our souls are invisible.** From birth to old age, through our daily lives and routines, we remain oblivious to it's presence. Unfortunately, when human beings are performing sinful deeds against others, they do not realize they are essentially destroying their own souls. The actions are reflected back onto themselves.

Through my spiritual awakening, I have recognized there is no need to seek retaliation against those who have wronged me. Reason being: The law of the Universe is equally fair. There is karma, or the saying: "What goes around, comes around," and other variations to this belief, the net result is the reflection of cause and effect. Therefore, I would never conceive of inflicting harm to anyone. If I do, I would be condemning myself for negative karma. Even negative counterproductive thoughts towards another being is poisonous to one's spirit.

In essence, you begin to heal yourself when you are able to reach this phase, and lead your soul to salvation. Wouldn't it be great if we were judged by our souls, true integrity, honesty, and not by our physical appearance, or the color of our skin? When you can judge a person by their true self, all else becomes irrelevant. For example, as an employer, I'd rather focus on the person's genuine character besides their scores, degrees, or references, based on my understanding, the sources can be fabricated. Our future leaders must be honest with a good sense of integrity to lead others, not the current CEO's who have greed within their heart's desire to mislead and deceive one another.

Have you sincerely analyzed yourself lately? Do you like what you see? First, visually erase your physical appearance completely, what remains is your soul; nothing else. If you dislike certain attributes of your character, you can change right now, this instant, not next year.

One path I have found through my journey is to maintain an absolute true sense of self. When you are genuine to yourself and others, your soul will surface to instruct you instinctively, in the difference between right and wrong, good and evil. Simple as that. Since birth your heart is basically pure, it will never fail, let you down, or betray you in any way. However, when you cloud yourself with deceit and lies, your spirit cannot forgive you. Thereby escalating a downward cycle towards the dismal route. A classic example, is that of a person who has committed a crime against someone. His conscience will not set him free, unconsciously he reveals his act to another person, without even realizing it.

Deceptive people are deep down emotionally inept, and are going towards a dark path. Their motive of thinking is the necessity to have an edge over others. Unbeknownst to them, the deception can only last so long. Eventually others will see right through them, then the game is over. The end result is: They are incriminating themselves, not others. The truth always surface in the end. Therefore, my motto is: "Honesty is the best route/action, the truth will set you free."

Before we can even begin to help others or society, I firmly believe we must heal ourselves. Everyone has their own foibles (weaknesses). No one is perfect on this planet, including myself. There are valid reasons to this. For your soul to fully achieve it's utmost potential towards the righteous path, it is vital to cleanse yourself of any addiction (tobacco, drugs, gambling, alcohol, sexual, etc.). Why? **An addictive personality of any form** is harmful to your spirit, whether it is physical or emotional. They contain roadblocks to your true purpose in life, robs you of insight, clarity, and clouds your judgment, towards the greater goals that your true soul aspires to become. Aside from leading the devastating vicious descending pursuits, this is affecting all those around, especially your loved ones. I feel it is quite tragic for human beings to depart from this earth. To become a contaminated lost soul, absent of any spirit, will, or hope.

In foresight, they are primarily mortally wounding themselves from achieving salvation. **We came into this world** with purity, good and kind hearts, devoid of any negative dimensions. **Along the way, we corrupt our souls** by imitating or learning immoral practices, associating with undesirable influences, or merely for the sake of fitting in. Rightfully, there is no one to blame, other than ourselves, due to the reasoning we are masters of our Universe. Forsake the disastrous cycles of self-hurt, the means are solely temporary measures.

Assert qualities of nurturing skills, to ascend towards the bright light, which we were meant, and destine to follow. The search for a beautiful life is totally within our reach. With steadfast dedication, the kind spirit will guide you in each phase of your journey.

In order to purify your soul, you must rid yourself of the dark forces that consume or surround your present state. Otherwise, this will control, and take possession of your entire life. Now, wouldn't it be appropriate to start with a clean slate? When you are riddled with doubts, fear, paranoia, one cannot proceed with those destructive behaviors. There is a Chinese proverb: "It takes three days to develop a habit, and three years to rid of it." We were born with free spirits, to allow ourselves to be impaired in such a way, the soul's original source of white light is in constant friction with the opposing evil powers. This prohibits the protective entity (spirit) in aiding the mortal being, whose sound decisions are besieged by unrelenting upheaval.

Why is it so difficult to rid ourselves the habitual traits? The solution is: "To find what ails us, and in order to dissolve our inner conflicts, we have to trace the dilemma to the original source." The exact cause could possibly be connected to the origins of our past childhoods, where a traumatic experience most likely invoke such an outcome. Those deep seeded wounds will surface into adulthood, and manifest as some self-compensatory mode of behavior.

Regardless, **since life is precious, it is most advantageous** for us to use our creative energies, to further improve our souls by extending harmony, and good will to mankind. This is the greatest gift to bestow upon ourselves. Becoming selfless and compassionate to others, is a benefit to the soul as well. Therefore, to have clarity (clear frame of mind) the possibilities are endless.

SUGGESTIONS FOR SELF-HEALING

"Natural Forces Within Us Are The True Healers Of Disease."
Hippocrates

CONVICTION + PERSEVERANCE = (+) RESULTS

A) CONVICTION

- Create a plan of action
- Make reachable short-term goals
- Remain committed in phases of failure

* Be strong!

B) PERSEVERANCE

- Do not give up
- Keep distractions at a minimum
- Maintain a clear vision of the outcome

* If you fall, get back on your feet!

C) (+) <u>RESULTS</u>

- **Light at the end of the tunnel**
- **New lease on life**
- **Make additional reforms on self-improvement**

* **Reward yourself!**

SUGGESTIONS FOR SELF-HEALING:

**The real strategy in dealing with any addictive behavior, is knowing why you do it in the first place, then you are on your way towards healing.

**Have faith in God or whatever religion you believe in. With God all things are possible.

**You owe it to yourself, no one is going to do it for you.

**When you think your situation is bleak, remember there is always someone worse than you.

**Do brief deep breathing exercises (they are relatively easy) to calm your inner self.

**Don't get mad, chew some gum for Christ's sake.

**Avoid blame, take responsibility for your own actions.

**Join support groups (AAA meetings, etc.).

**Keep a journal of your progress, this will help to evaluate yourself.

**A meditation class or hobby can foster positive outcome, and letting go of negative habits.

**No matter how dire your state is, ask the True Source/God for healing.

POEM

A Depressed State of Mind

Suddenly my world became dark and blue
To which I vaguely have a clue

There seems to be no rhyme or reason
When this appears amidst the seasons

I feel sad, vulnerable, and weak
There's a desperate solution for which I seek

All the while, I just want to cry
I just keep asking myself why?

I ask almighty God for help
But all I could do is yelp

Nothing at the moment makes sense
Which even makes me more tense

I've got to snap out of this state of mind
Deep down it's serenity I wish to find

The release of pent-up emotions brings relief
Armed with courage, I am no longer weak

CHAPTER TWO

NURTURING YOUR SOUL

Star Wars: "May the force be with you."

Our soul is the most vital everlasting commodity. We must treasure, and preserve it's wholeness as much as possible. More importantly, this invaluable entity is crucial to our existence as a being. Besides, it is invisible to ourselves, and everyone. Without it our life would be empty, meaningless, and lacking fruition. **How do you preserve your soul?** One needs to make a conscious effort to follow the correct way in life, obey society's rules, and nurture our inner soul. To do so, requires daily mental regimens, aimed continuously in a lifetime goal of counteracting the dark forces, that bombard our daily lives. Keep in mind, the evil nature is constantly lurking to uncover your moments of weakness, will seize with haste to trap, and capture your irreplaceable soul.

The devil is merciless, in his **ever unyielding attempts to ensnare,** and lure you into the dark kingdom of no return. He knows your frailties and vulnerabilities. We all possess a dual right /wrong side to our personality, and decision-making. When one is confronted with a diabolical or intense situation, train yourself to not allow the dark nature overtake you. For instance, the undesirable mind will provide permission: "Go ahead, do it, no one is looking."

When this thought process appears, immediately utilize your positive forces to remind yourself with: "There are consequences which will affect me, and my significant others as well, it is not worth the effort, and walk away."

This mental exercise is a valuable tool, to extricate or disengage those hidden demons, which dwells within us. When the rewards are so tempting to resist, take a deep breath, and brief moment to contemplate the outcome. If it is excruciatingly irresistible to you, take time to say a prayer to God for guidance, in your decision-making. Do not on all accounts make a hasty verdict, one false or wrong move can be an irretrievable mistake.

Another practical approach often neglected when unforeseen circumstances strike, is utilizing the common sense method. How often is it most vulnerable when we are caught off-guard, especially when we least expect it? Again, ask yourself the possible foreseen outcome: A permanent criminal record, punishment, everlasting guilt/shame, and being ostracized from society.

Applying practical safe judgment, can defeat the negative urges surrounding our desires. Although it does not guarantee success each time. When the individual is already weak, and have fallen prey other times, even the best reasonable decisions may not prevail. This is precisely why I suggest you consistently train yourself, to offset any impending traps (the illusions of sin). **Common sense is an alert mechanism, whereby your inner reasoning takes over,** rather than with impulsive behavior. It requires being attentive to recognize such moments, and intervene with purposeful caution.

Furthermore, **a human's basic weakness,** is that he deludes himself into thinking he will escape from it. Little does he know, the **law of the Universe is undeniably fair, the end justifies the means.** For example, a common error everyone makes is speeding or DUI, they are aware of the pitfalls, sometimes wrought with tragic consequences. Yet, they continue with these actions. You may elude detection once or twice, eventually fate catches up to you.

One of the deadly demonic forces that confronts us constantly, is greed. We live in a culture of have and have nots. This further perpetuates those with frail mindsets to gravitate, attain and pursue at all costs, including their valuable souls. When the hearts of men or women are comprised of greed, it will siphon the essence/wholeness out of their souls, gradually and insidiously to the unending desire of more gluttony, in the eventual demise of their individual path, upon self-destruction.

What is gained through deceit, ill-gotten gains, and dishonorable means will have a zero net worth because it was not self-earned. This is the **principle Universal concept.** One of the profound devastating effects of the dark side- you become blind-sighted, impervious to the red flags, and sound advice of others.

The tactic I have used most of my life and **advice to others:** <u>"Surround yourself with upstanding individuals with sound morals,</u> who do not possess ulterior motives for their own selfish means." I will not hesitate to say, it is difficult nowadays for me to find quality people. Especially for a minority, such as myself. We live in closed gated communities, often with our guards up. In all my fifty-two years, I have yet to meet a truly genuine hearted person (aside from my husband), the ones I've encountered have left me with a bitter taste.

Coincidentally, **the priests and deacons I have come upon, with their extensive theology and spiritual knowledge, have left me greatly disappointed.** I find their philosophies and the theological connections lacking. I have seened their souls, some are lost in their own selfish objectives, and also striving to uncover true purpose in life. On the contrary, I am not against the clerics or the Catholic establishment. This is my honest assessment of them. Despite all this, I will always respect these individuals as representatives of God.

To illustrate my disappointments, I have rational reasons to back my claims. For instance, **I will never discuss racism topics with a priest or deacon again, for they truly miss the mark on sensitivity,** the damaging life-long changing, and profound effects it has on me. During one occasion, I went out of my comfort zone, and offered unconditionally my free services, to volunteer at a nun's retirement home. "Call back in one year," was the reply. Determined, I personally appealed to the Mother Superior in honest integrity, with similar outcome. I felt like a dejected human being with no love from my parents, as well as from the church. This apparent episode affected me for awhile, but not for long. I continued to perform good deeds in other means, since my love for God is immense.

This love (for True Source- God) is eternal to the deepest core of my soul, with the loyalty pledge of everlasting goodwill till my last breath. Time and again, I am being tested for my faith and belief in him. This is what I know, **true devotion lies within one's inner heart and deeds, with the utmost sincerity, void of ego, recognition, or acknowledgment.**

Suffice to say, I am quite certain honest souls exists amongst us, I have not been fortunate enough to meet one. There are kind individuals in all shapes and sizes, especially the overly obese population, for they are yearning to contribute productively, yet are often rejected because of others' sheer stupidity and ignorance. To me, I see them as the teddy bears of the world, with boundless love to offer, if society could accept them for who they are. Therefore, I offer my heart-felt empathy in their struggles to belong, and fit in. **The harsh reality is,** we are judged mainly on appearances alone, rather than worthiness and sincere intentions. Thankfully, we have movies such as "Shrek" to remind us <u>true beauty lies from within, not on the surface.</u>

The ramifications of rejection is devastating to one's spirit. The sense of being accepted nurtures the soul. The sense of belonging is fundamental to the existence of our being. One of the side effects of in-acceptance, is that we all become withdrawn, closed in, even shut ourselves out from others. <u>The hurt and pain are too unbearable.</u> We begin to live in our own world, blame ourselves, and consuming our empty shell with undesirable habits, live in seclusion, sedentary lifestyles, overeating, etc. The remedy for rejection, either from society or loved ones is: **"Find peace within yourself, and disregard their hurtful remarks."** Many times, I needed to remind myself it was not my fault entirely, in fact their problem to begin with. There is a saying: "You cannot please everyone," is a true essence of the very word.

Obliterate those harmful habits, and invent healthy outlets (exercise, hobbies, etc.). I have often used solitude for solace in finding my inner peace, when conflicting thoughts confuse the logical side of the mind. I escape to my garden, and connect with nature, for the answers suddenly appear coherently within me. Find your niche, whatever works for you, and develop mental/spiritual strength to sustain your soul.

The emphasis I would like to make, is be kind to your soul, have a periodic reminder of the entity, and treasure it. Consider the resource as your gateway to heaven or enlightenment. **How can you be kind to your soul?** Very simple. **It encompasses all the deeds you have exhibited throughout your daily life.** Resulting in a reciprocal effect, kind acts warrant bright outcomes, corrupt actions have negative results.

The ill-will hearted often conceive they have the upper hand. Actually, it happens to be the opposite. The good natured ones, in reality have won. In the end, their souls remained whole and intact. **Case in point: I was enrolled in Catholic elementary school.** This event occurred in first grade. **One day** my brother and I were walking in the hallway. Suddenly, we came across a $20.00 bill. In those days (1960's), it was considered a large sum. Keeping the money never crossed our minds, even though we lived in a laundry, and we were poor ourselves. Without hesitation, we immediately returned the bill to the office. Days later, the principal thanked my mother for our kindness.

Another example of a kind act is true-sharing. In college, I commuted via the subway system. This was in Manhattan, New York. I was waiting at the platform for the train. A young man in his thirties approached me, a total stranger I have never met. He asked me for five dollars, simply because he needed it, that was his explanation. I had only $5.00 in my pocket, it was lunch money my mom provided me for the entire day. I asked if he could repay me later, if I agreed. He promised verbally he would, and even volunteered to write down his address on my note pad.

The sympathy for this stranger, overcame my fears of hunger, or my own needs. I had hoped on his integrity to keep his word, and freely gave him the money. The woman standing close by, had a weary expression on her face. Then he left. By lunch time, I was hungry. I borrowed money from a classmate, and promised to repay her. I paid her the following day in class.

Incidentally, I never heard from the stranger, he rescinded on his promise. I felt stupid, and foolish at the time for trusting him. I do not regret my actions to this day. Fast forward thirty years later, I now believe my kind deeds have assisted me in achieving wisdom, knowledge, and insight. Without those acts, I am not where I am today.

The more good deeds you perform consistently on a persistent basis, the will of your heart can further perpetuate greater resiliency into other avenues. These actions will continue to nurture your soul. By the same token, it is unnecessary to go out of your way to commit acts of kindness. Mine just happened out of nowhere. When the wish is not genuine, it nullifies and voids the act itself.

When a person becomes pretentious, he or she is merely masking their false motives, resulting in bad outcomes. As a child, **my mother** had a tendency to kneel in front of the church steps, and gesturing a sign of the cross. Too afraid to make a comment, I knew in my heart she was a great con artist in disguise. She would **randomly inflict physical pain on me and my brother,** shoplift, and swindled. I had to suffer in deep silence, knowing all the while her misdeeds were immoral, it disturbed me tremendously.

****

****

BADGE OF COURAGE

*****Honor To Thyself*****

Arm Thyself With An Impenetrable Body Armor, & Shield. Develop An Iron-will/ Resistance, To Withstand Whatever Life Offers You.

****

YOU CANNOT LET YOURSELF DOWN!

****

This Is Your Eternal Pledge, To Defend Against The Elements, & For Living.

****

****

<u>METHODS TO NURTURE YOUR SOUL</u>

A. <u>Reform Yourself</u>

As humans, we all have the basic concept of right and wrong, irregardless of IQ. There are no exceptions to gender, status, or ethnicity. The only ones excused are the mentally handicapped, or borned without the ability to think. We all make mistakes, including myself. This is a fact of life. How you retrieve, and recover from those ill-encounters will shape, mold, and alter your ultimate fate, or destiny until eternity. Yes, eternity sounds forever, and is a very long time.

It is important to make provisions for any unforeseen outcomes, that may arise out of nowhere. We need to devise strategic lifetime goals for ourselves to make it there. For that reason alone, it is never outlandish to formulate ahead a plan, for the lengthy voyage in our redemption. An authentic concerted effort, is necessary for true success.

<u>Reforming your ways-</u> can be manifested in many different approaches. Consciously, ask yourself what needs improvement in your personal life. The initiative to advance as a human being is not easily accomplished. We frequently have countless temptations surrounding our endeavors, in a self-fulfilling prophecy towards failure. **Utilize determination to accept your faults or downfalls.** Amend those mistakes before they escalate any further. Next, take appropriate action to rectify them, because no one is going to do it for you.

Then, there are those who lack moral values, or the vision to admit their own deficits, which alludes them in behaving a certain way, day after day. I am commenting regarding the constant little lies, humans voice on a daily basis. Naturally, how can one even begin to nurture his or her soul when you perpetrate this? **The act of lying prevents the spirit from progressing.** Imagine lying once or twice a day, then multiply the amount in a year, into a lifetime accumulation of lies. Essentially, the soul is being systematically reduced to the point of no return, by the continual cyclical (cycle) pattern of deceptions, leading to a dark abyss from it's original form (pure state). Thus, **disabling the soul's labyrinth (inter-connected passage) of continuation.**

For instance, my mom has a life-long habitual behavior of deceit towards me, and others. She has lied too often. I believe half of the time, she is oblivious to her own lying. I had confronted my mother, sadly she chose denial, and silence on her part. Unfortunately, this is a direct result of the devil's treacherous entrapment of one's soul, condemning it into further doom.

One of the ways I reformed myself, was with my shopping excursions. Granted, I have always maintained within my means, never exceeding the budget. Initially, this all started when I was in college. I was miserable, and unhappy with my life. No love from my mother, and conflicts with identity issues. I compensated by buying whenever I was disappointed, or sad, through rational excuses I made for myself. Even though I was not working, I utilized money from the nursing student loan to alleviate my depressed moods. Fortunately, my spending did not escalate. I paid off every monthly credit card bill.

Throughout my marriage, I continued to purchase within my means. I began to concede the shopping was controlling me, not vice versa. I came to the realization that I could no longer justify my unsubstantiated reckless spending, my underlying problems were still unresolved, but merely masked by short-term gratifications. I had to stop. As an intervention, I cancelled all my credit cards, except those for essentials, and credit history. Afterwards, I felt a weight had lifted from my shoulders. From that point on, I had my life back in control.

Finally, this enabled me to concentrate on pursuing more resourceful goals, and valuable interests. I did not return to my old ways. Clearly, **I made a significant decision, and choice to annihilate the strong-hold attachments.** Having the release of this burden, has inspired me to appreciate how fortunate I am, and be grateful for my situation. Knowing there are millions in third world countries, who are less fortunate than me.

B. Clean Your Slate

Life often comes with difficult challenges, to offset and derail our courses. The proper protocol is admitting to our individual failures/ mistakes, and make restitutions for them. The important facet of nurturing the soul, is **minimizing the accumulation of sins piled against one's soul.** It's so critical for our on-going spiritual growth. This relevance, and reasoning cannot be undermined with trivial careless undertaking.

The more you retain the wholesomeness of your soul, the greater cognizance (awareness) you will become in achieving your long-term objectives. The serious consequences of your actions determines the future course of your soul.

Far too often, we are preoccupied with non-essential concerns, surrounding our daily living (materialistic pleasures). We place ourselves in unnecessary risks, without the full gravity of the situation taken into perspective (road rage, an alcohol induced state), all for the immediate responses to our unprepared nature. The multitude of offenses add considerable weight to your soul, further deepening it's despair.

How do you repair damage to you soul? One goal at a time, it cannot be completed overnight. **Having knowledge, is the first insight in resolving the underlying problem.** Instituting long-term doable intentions, is heading in the right direction. Furthermore, once you omit one sin, it is foremost not to repeat the pattern again. This must be initiated in utmost integrity of your heart, otherwise it will become a complete waste of time. We are all creatures of habit, exercise awareness to break the cycle of repeated mistakes, and remorseful acts. First, **acknowledge the sin. Submit to yourself the action was wrong, then make an assessment to prevent the domino effect.**

When I was six years old, my mom conducted her weekly grocery shopping every Sunday, in Chinatown (New York City). My mother was not an honest woman, she usually pilfers whatever she could get her hands on. Prior to entering the premises, I was instructed on cue to walk in front of her, and wait there. This routine continued, until I could no longer masquerade the act. At the time, I had no inclinations of my actions. I was simply a child then, I had to comply, and listen. Otherwise, **I was fearful of ritually being beaten with metal hangers.**

During adolescence, the inner thoughts remained in my mind. Throughout adulthood, the heavy sins of the past took a toll on the well-being of my soul. Even though I did not masterminded those episodes of shoplifting, I became guilt-ridden. My conscience unrelentlessly reminded me, from time to time. Finally, in my mid-thirties, I could not ignore the emotional burden any longer. The will for closure, was the antidote to end my misery.

One day while in Chinatown with my mom, I confided to her. **I intended to return to the shop, where I stole as a young child. To repay, and ask for forgiveness from the owner.** My mom's irrepressible reactions, were of total shock, disbelief, and disgust. She further implied I would be a disgrace, and shame to her reputation, made repeated despicable facial expressions, and continued disparaging statements, in an attempt to hinder my endeavors. Her offensive nasty remarks, did not sway me in the least bit. In fact, I was more determined to complete my mission. I motioned a time frame to meet my mother later, when this was over.

I was quite nervous, and a little apprehensive that day. Nevertheless, I had to accomplish this. Something instinctive in my heart, **propelled me to go ahead without any fear.** I asked for the owner, greeted her privately, and confessed to my crimes. I genuinely poured my emotions out to this woman, with tears rolling down my face, asking forgiveness, and to repay her. All I had was $50.00 at the time, she accepted $25.00. That was it. She commented: "It wasn't your fault."

I reunited with my mother, and she suddenly admitted: "You did the right thing." Following this incident, **I became whole again, felt reconnected, and reborn.** The person I offended forgave me. That meant more to me than anything else in the whole world, priceless! No amount of therapy, could possibly resolve the pain and agony, from the sins of my past.

A year later, I realized the grocery owner had sold her business. In hindsight, this was an uneasy endeavor. I had accumulated a great deal of shame with my grief. I seized the right pivotal moment to complete the task, otherwise the chances, or opportunity for redemption might have been missed. To this day, I breathe with a sigh of relief. **It paved the way for my recovery into other avenues of cleansing my sins, garnering, and reaping greater benefits of wisdom, knowledge, and insight.**

As you can see, **it is never too late to remove sins from the past.** Tell yourself, fear is not an option. Another form of purifying your slate is through confession, or whatever religious institution you belong to, and genuinely repent those sins. **True remorse is the initial phase of self-redemption.** The next step is to retain your promise. Till the end of your lifetime.

Perhaps this is the most arduous of all. **Can you prevent temptation from surfacing again?** Have a backup plan to avoid it. Reward yourself with each successful attempt. If you had done a terrible misdeed with the involved party, return to make amends. Express your deep sorrow, and make restitutions with the individual. The primary goal- is to ask for forgiveness.

Bear in mind. Once you commit to a promise, and repeat the violation at another point in time, the oath becomes null and void. Bad deeds will omit the good deeds. Hence, proceed with caution and vigilance of not misguiding oneself. In essence, the **repercussion of any one action** has a direct influence into present, and future circumstances. Since the lifetime cycle has never progressed or improved, the being will continue on this pattern into his next journey. In contrast, positive attributes will garner greater conditions. Only then, the wheel of destiny advances to a better state, in order for true redemption to take place. In addition, take in consideration other faults that harbors your soul, one is held accountable for every action in life.

We live in a world inundated with sex, violence, vividly portrayed through television, movies, and internet exposures. A person cannot clean their slate, if he or she continually bombard themselves with these kind of influences. Unbeknownst to the viewers, **with exhibition of violent acts, there are underlying subliminal messages being emitted into their subconscious minds.** The calm conscious awareness becomes unapparent to the thinking state of mind.

For example, we often lose our tempers at the worst inexplicable moments. **There is a dual side to everyone's psyche (mind).** When the thought process is consistently conditioned with aggression and negativity, the dark side will overtake and control your good nature, in preventing you to arrive at an amicable standpoint. The diabolical forces, inevitably will condone your reasoning towards further escalation, spitefulness, or retaliation. Which explains why certain individuals cannot recall their actions rationally, only till after the fact. They become blank in offering detailed explanations, of what propelled them to react at the particular situation.

Case in point: There are televised documented testimonials, of victims afflicted with sexual addiction. Their suffering started innocently enough, through visual browsing of porn web sites. They gradually increased their eventual insatiable compulsion, because **those subliminal messages were instilling permissive behaviors of-** excitement, allure, immediate sense of gratification, and delusions of harmless fantasy.

I wish to implore individuals with an already weakened sense of self, to avoid the negative world we live in today. My hope for you is to retain the good, and positive behaviors which dwells within you. Do not be swayed or seduced by instant indulgences. Their intended motive is to have a sole purpose, to claim your soul to the depths of condemnation.

Fortunately, <u>I grew up in the Walt Disney era of goody two shoes. Yippee!</u> It was a glorious period, which I cherished and loved. Those old movies promoted good values of integrity, righteousness, and wholesome entertainment. Also, **I love Mickey Mouse!** Even till this day, I relish those memories. What is remarkable, **the torch of innocence continues to burn deep inside of me.** I will strive with diligent efforts to be a kind, honest, compassionate human being to others. For that flame never ceases, embedded into my daily thinking, it has empowered me to do random acts of good-will, forgive others (very difficult), and continually nurture my soul towards reception of advancing wisdom, and deeper insights into the sacred realm (kingdom).

This empowerment is profound, and real in every fiber of my being. Having the insight of retaining a child-like mind and pure thinking, has further elevated my spiritual acuity to a heightened level of religious connectedness with almighty God. To my humblest humility to God, I will be a faithful servant to him, that is my everlasting pledge.

C. <u>Connect With Spirituality</u>

I cannot begin to tell you, how my spirituality has altered every aspect of analytical reasoning, concept, and belief system. **Faith is a powerful and effective element in nurturing one's soul.** It sets you on a right direction, and to persevere in the path towards the "light," away from evil. Trust in God, has kept me grounded most of my life. Otherwise, I would have floundered into a state of non-purposeful ambitions, goals, and erroneous decisions.

There are many ways to communicate with God, one of them is through consistent prayer. Not when you are primarily in dire straits. It's during normal activities, genuine heart-felt intentions, towards a deeper sense of real thought, and meaning with the Lord. **Humans have a tendency of neglecting God, when normalcy reigns.** However, when one's health or predicament is unexpectedly endangered, with a life threatening crisis or disease. They flock to church, ask God for a cure, and to immediately intervene on their behalf. This is not how faith works.

How would you feel, if someone only came to you in times of urgency, and expect a miracle? Afterwards, ignores you when everything is fine? I am not implying, God will reject those who seek him solely in times of need. On the contrary, he consists of love, and compassion for all of us. I need you to **ponder the significance of spirituality.** Will your faith wane into despair when the prayers are unanswered? Or recognize, this is simply a passage of time, and events. Aimed at testing your true commitment with almighty Father, despite all the negative outcomes.

A high ranking New York Buddhist monk remarked on C-Span: " It is more important to know the meaning of life than going to church." To me, it is unnecessary to go through the motions of attending mass, for the sake of pretending to be a good Christian. While your heart is merciless towards others, and being totally oblivious to the ramifications of reality. The act you portray simply defeats the purpose itself, in a futile attempt to deceive, and mask thyself to impress others. I believe this is a betrayal to one's soul (for it is based entirely on truth), whereas your actions are a complete waste of valuable time.

Since **we are all ingrained with flaws within ourselves,** I need to confess. My faith was not strong towards God, during my tumultuous thirties. It was a period of immense anger, pain, resentment (from my past), confusion, and the sense of unfairness. In that injustice, I blamed God conveniently for all the problems I had encountered. This was a time of great upheaval. My husband and I had left New York. We relocated to Arizona. He was obligated to fulfill his scholarship, as pay-back. The early years were spent on a desolate, isolated Indian reservation, away from civilization. I had no one I could converse with, or confide in. Consequently, through lengthy soul searching, I could no longer shift the blame onto anyone (especially God). **Truthfully, I am responsible for my own actions.**

The solid choices we decide on, create a major impact, and form those crucial formidable enforcements to join, and unite with God. I made a critical decision in time, to make peace with him, for God is not the enemy. I was struggling within myself. Amidst my deepened misery of despair and hopelessness, the net entangled me into an enclosed web, preventing my path towards clarity, resolution, and self-help. Somehow the spirit guided me, in the tunnel of darkness.

I can divulge to everyone in unquestionable faith. **Once you create that holy bond with God, it becomes an unbreakable, unimaginable consoling fortress, which surrounds one with serenity, peace, and a sound presence.** This feeling pervades, over whatever the surmounting situation appears, to be at the time. It has takened me, over half a lifetime to acquire this. Faith is not given to you, it has to be earned. There were countless times where my faith have been tested.

Having faith within one's inner soul, is similar to obtaining absolute truth. Eliminating the slightest amount of doubt, and indecision into the nature of your problems. You become reconciled, and in-peace mentally. **Not directed towards self-blame or others, rather acceptance of the eventual outcome.** This is how true spirituality speaks to me. I am focused with God as a whole, to analyze the perplex circumstances at hand. To confidently know it is God's will, whatever the end result is, there must be a purposeful intent and rationale for the occurrence.

I would like to share a story of how my faith was tested. I befriended an Asian woman. One day, she verbally attacked me with a very offensive remark. It hurt me deeply at the time, for I was kind to her, and this is how she showed her gratitude. I felt complete disgust, betrayal, and couldn't overcome my grief-strickened mentality. I had nowhere to go, no support system, or anyone to confide with. At that instant, I quickly assessed my course of action. I droved to the vacant church parking lot, all alone. As I sat inside my car, I cried and poured my heart out to the Lord. Revealing my simultaneous childhood pain, which surfaces whenever I am vulnerable, and hurt. Even though no one heard me, I was on sacred grounds.

In my heart, **I was cognizant the Saints were attentive to my presence,** and they heard my distress. Incidentally, the church doors were closed in the evening. At the time, I had absolutely no shred of doubt in my mind, or even questioned the rationale of my behavior. I was there for almost an hour. I comprehended this was a testimonial of my true spiritual faith. Which propelled my will and desire, to confront my weaknesses/moment of angst, and connect with God, instead of masking the problems.

When panic overtakes your senses, especially when one is all alone, you instantly feel defenseless against the elements. In a time when I could not trust anyone, that incident changed my life dramatically, because God tested my faith during an important pivotal, vulnerable core of my being. This was one of the challenging trials that were placed upon me. I was unaware of the situation at hand, yet I was able **to prove my sincerity and worthiness to God, as an imperfect fragile human being.** By exposing my true self. This exemplified my honest intentions of believing God implicitly.

I wholeheartedly encourage anyone, whatever their religion, to visit a holy place, temple, or synagogue, to find solace in nurturing their soul. I cannot emphasize enough for myself, what it is to be in peace with the almighty Father, and allow him to comfort, and implant belief into my presence, that I am not alone in this chaotic world. The True Source will become a sanctity for your erratic reasoning, and the misguided treacherous distractions, that may prevail upon you.

In my mid-twenties, when I felt lost or bewildered, I would escape to a nearby Catholic church, and prayed. It has, and always will be a sanctuary for my soul. There, I can ascertain ultimate quietude within the depths of my soul. To obtain meaning, and further evaluate the purpose of my daily existence. Especially to acquire the virtues of contentment, in perspective to others in worse predicaments. From that point, I can appreciate the plight of events. With this belief system, my reason on this earth has a broader message. I can attain this understanding, to incorporate it into further spiritual growth. **And advancement towards greater self-awareness, within the deep spiritual spheres of accelerated knowledge/wisdom attainment.**

This is what the great holy gurus, and sages have known for centuries. In their quest for the special gifts of any spiritual advancement, they all have an unconditional bond with the True Source (God, Buddha, Allah, etc.). Conviction in your individual faith, is the utmost requisite for exhibiting loyalty in one's religion. Consistent daily conscious awareness of faith, has reinforced my comprehension of the immense complexity of our Universe. With the knowledge I have retained, it has enabled me to plan, and execute my course for life. Most notably, definite repetitive patterns re-occur in our lives. This confirms how well each of us master the lessons, adapt, and achieve resolution of formidable challenges, that comes our way.

To demonstrate one's abilities and will-power, those unexplained events conveniently surface out of nowhere, in awkward situations. **Our endurance, or tolerance towards the prevailing circumstances, are all determinations of our true character as revealed to God.**

D. The Power of Compassion

As an Asian-American, **I suffered all the insults, racial slurs, discriminations, and injustices.** I am not immune from my fellow Asian foreigners, with their unwarranted rude comments about me. There is a Chinese proverb: **"One day of patience, equals one hundred days of fortune."** I now understand (from my resilience) I am noteworthy in God's eyes. The affirmations are a blessing in disguise. Being a minority, the criterions placed on me are stringent.

In my early twenties, I experienced an identity crisis. I felt disconnected in the American culture, with no sense of belonging. All the years of society's abuses, have taken a toll on my psychological well-being. At times, **I wished I was Caucasian,** dismissing my true heritage, while continuously being anchored by my roots and ancestry.

Gradually, I realized these fantasies were a temporary quick-fix. I needed to retain my genuine self for any real solutions to emerge, and resolve my dilemma. Having a concept of right and wrong, it was apparent that the hatred being thrust upon me, was a dark force aimed at inducing hate from within myself.

I have made a vow with God, each time someone offends me in any fashion, I will forgive the other person. In order to counter the wicked forces, I essentially took it a step further, by extending mercy to the individual. Precaution warns me: **"I must not venture to their level, for this will be my greatest defeat."** I have a challenge for other minorities as well: "Can you look upon your enemies with forgiveness and compassion?" Know that you were placed on this earth for a given task.

Do not give into animosity, with spite in return. Then you would have failed, and only succeeded in entering the dark path, which fuels the bitterness even more. The disease of hatred will manifest into a form of cancer, invading and impeding spiritual growth, thereby halting any chance of progress.

It is counterproductive to nurture the soul, while harboring hurtful thoughts against others. It will be a futile attempt to merge into the spiritual world, for God is synonymous with love, and compassion. Remove those detestable thoughts from your mind, they are the source of burden to one's soul, causing further delay in any break for spiritual improvement; including awakening the wisdom within you.

Forgiving others is a very difficult task. **If you can, then you have prevailed.** There is nothing complicated about this. It is quite simple, yet arduous to fulfill. During the trials and tribulations of our daily lives, compassion is often the most challenging to perform. This trait is not inherent in all of us, which requires continuous practice over the course of everyone's lifetime.

My spiritual achievements have been a culmination of life-long good deeds, forgiveness, and treating others with kindness, which at times, tested my genuine intentions to the highest degree. I can tell you this, once you become accustomed to completing good deeds, there is a natural sense of elation that surrounds you. Your endorphins, and energy levels increases as well, from those kind acts.

Compassion has to be real, not a masquerading act, or ploy to deceive yourself and others. Having sympathy, is a required trait to execute your actions. Hence, these repetitive behaviors will procure your state of mind in the direction of God's kingdom, aspiring the role of "truth seeker." When you become an instrumental force in the alliance with God, inevitably good outcomes will surface into one's life. In actuality, while helping others, you are saving your own soul. Once you have achieved a kind kindred spirit, it can sustain you especially during the dark moments of despair.

From my personal experience of performing a lifetime of benevolent deeds, I can honestly attest, **compassion is the source to obtaining infinite true wisdom.** This is far beyond the beginning levels of wisdom, it is the final step in the process of deep spiritual awakening. This is the most burdensome position to achieve, let alone for non-believers to comprehend. Reaching this stage, demands at least half a lifetime's dedication of compassion, true intentions, pure mind-spirit attributes, personal sacrifices, non-prejudicial views of others, and a total inner-core soul declaration to God.

The gift of true wisdom power is contingent, and subjective to God's decision alone, those who are worthy to receive. The trials given to each individual extends beyond will, mind, and spirit matters, for anyone to strive in the advance phases of great all-knowing wisdom. I am truly grateful to God for this knowledge. The reason is, for another person, it may necessitate indefinite life journeys to attain.

Acquiring humility and showing mutual respect, is a beneficial attribute to have in receptiveness, towards reaching spiritual awareness. The insights he or she wishes to seek, will not be apparent to those who are greedy or ambitious in attaining their goals. Be mindful of your good purpose, the rest will follow accordingly, to the sequence of chain events. All spiritual journeys are pre-destined to fate, cause, and effect (deeds), sincerity of heart in the righteous path. Most importantly, void of compulsion in any form.

Remember, any form of addiction will set your life's cycle backwards, not forward. Humility is one of the secret ingredients in mastering deeper virtues of true compassion, which encompasses heart/mind/Godly intentions, in the sincerest form.

All the Saints were humans, before attaining Sainthood. **The common trait was** their surpassed dedication of compassion, and love towards every living creature on this earth. Anyone, including myself can find inspiration, to share the God-like qualities, and follow in their direction, to be accepted as a divine spirit in God's heavenly kingdom. Do not expect miracles in your destiny, proceed in a natural manner. Relinquish an ambitious mindset, for you will not find it. **Reward gravitates to those with pure hearts.**

Another commonality among Saints, is that they did not possess high IQ's, therefore irrelevant to intelligence. What they acquired were natural powers of advance spiritual understanding, capacity of complete devotion to God. While embracing and practicing daily virtues of humility, selfless acts of kindness, and their unyielding profound actions in serving humanity. **The holy Saints** (such as Padre Pio, and Saint Faustina), have served as role models for me. To follow in their path, and aspire to gain a heightened level of awareness.

I encourage everyone to allow God's spirit to flow into their hearts. **Thereby, enlighten each wisdom towards eventual self-redemption of the soul, for that is the meaning of life.** I may not succeed in entering heaven in this life. However, once I am determined to navigate that direction, I believe my devotion, and unending love for God will pave the way for me, in the blessed kingdom that awaits me.

There are ways to acquire a sense of compassion within oneself. First, develop a simple way of thinking, void of any outsmarting or maneuvering behaviors. Place yourself in other people's situations, comprehend their pain and suffering. Develop sympathetic views, as if it was your own predicament, and the ramification of the situation. Practicing this frame of reasoning can establish additional merits. These intuitions will develop feelings of gratitude, and to view the world with open-mindedness. The other **powerful asset of compassion,** is the inclination of harboring lower importance of material possessions.

Once you have attained the acts of kindness, your attention is directed to the greater causes of humanity, rather than the worthless cycle of self-absorption. These endearing behaviors will enhance your desire for other charitable causes, such as volunteering, or donating to a charity, etc. In effect, **decreasing the unnecessary burdens** (or indulgences). Unknowingly, and indirectly being placed upon ourselves.

Beware of temptations, arrows and daggers aimed at misguiding you off-course. These include family, friends, associates, neighbors, and even those we trust. Always trust yourself first, your instincts, and feelings. Others may perceive our compassion as a gullibility factor, thereby taking advantage of us. Be discerning in who you trust, and share information with. Those exact friends, can possibly become your worst enemies.

A classic example, is when I regularly donate to my Catholic charities. I am immediately placed on a roster mailing list of the other agencies, eager to accept my contributions. I would receive, as many as two mailings in one day. Often, I am not familiar with these charitable organizations. Naturally I discard the rest. Some may not be reliable or reputable at all, merely scams to solicit your hard-earned money.

Unbeknownst to most everyone, the exceptional power of continual compassion is gaining good karma, and outcomes for oneself. In Hinduism and Buddhism, **Karma is described as the sum, and the consequences of a person's action during the successive phases of his existence, regarded as determining one's fate.** Every notable accomplishment accrued from the present condition, will be carried onto his or her next journey.

I also firmly believe you can alter your current destiny, into a more harmonious outcome. Although it may not be as altogether drastic, certainly anyone can change their fate in life through compassion. Why? Simply put- **the realm of karma is fair, what you put forward, becomes an added advantage in return.** Similarly, deplorable acts also manifest unfortunate results, no matter how clever, or elaborate the plot was. The end always justifies the means. Specifically why I dislike when someone attempts to outwit others, only to ruined themselves in the final end.

This is more the reason I advocate performing charitable deeds, to assure preservation of my soul, and gathering acute spiritual knowledge, towards achieving intuitive wisdom. **There are gradual levels in seeking wisdom,** it is derived naturally in various stages, no set point in time. You will know, once the source of information is acquired. Do not anticipate the arrival of future spiritual concepts, this is hindering the process.

One day while at home, my "wisdom" warned me of an impending danger concerning my husband. He was out on errands. For no reason, I immediately uttered a prayer: "The Our Father." When my husband arrived, I inquired whether he had encountered any disaster on his way back. He mentioned he almost had a collision with another vehicle, just blocks from our residence, and was abled to instantly brake in time, to prevent an accident. It became abundantly clear to us, the incident occurred at the exact time I had prayed. God's Angels intervened. This is how "wisdom" inexplicably performs miracles. There is no rhyme or reason to this power, once you have tapped into it. **Wisdom can literally derail a perilous predicament, and save your life.**

E. FOOD FOR THE SOUL

1) Love

Love is a fundamental quintessential necessity for mankind's survival, and to nourish one's soul. Without it, we become incomplete, less than whole. Life seems meaningless, to go forward with our future endeavors. **Love is also a very powerful emotion, that can allow our spirits to soar to the highest atmosphere,** or wreck havoc. Bring forth hellish brutal mental anguish, or consequences to our entire existence. Lust, jealousy, and love's mixture can be a detrimental combination to one's soul.

Such feelings can lead to devastating results, to modify his or her fate. Therefore, it is wise to be cautious in choosing a soul mate. Finding a mate is half the battle, expect tumultuous paths to navigate in the distance.

When the right person comes along, love is **a vital asset to nurture each others soul,** to grow in unison, from all those shared experiences. Evidence to support this are the published findings. Married couples outlived single individuals, in terms of life span, and longevity. The bonding process encourages endearing feelings of wanting to live, for the sake of the partner. Along with the endurance to remain with each other, through wonderful, and challenging times.

This is what sustains the hearts and minds of the human race, to face adversity with awe-inspiring determination and will-power. Additionally, the common factor amongst relationships who have endured twenty-five years or longer, were traits of forgiveness, understanding, and compromise.

Nowadays, the divorce rate is alarmingly high, all due to lack of patience, selfish needs, and desires. Most importantly, the inability to be truthful with one another. Tainted with the mask of false pretenses, and the stubborn unwillingness to surrender one's position, of absolute right and wrong.

When I came into this world, I chose the most excruciating journey of all- no love. **In the absence of love,** a person becomes incapacitated, and frightened within the context of purpose. **To interpret this: "The conscious heart that dwells within, realistically, and automatically responds. To absorb the hollow existential (existing) emotional state, of non-acceptance from this world. Which makes us feel unloved."** Throughout my life, I was hopelessly lost, from the lack of love of my parents. This affected every aspect of my mental well-being, and behavior. The resounding side effects of this, ultimately impacted me dramatically- non-trust in others, inability to deal with stress, poor nutrition, loss of confidence and being petrified, when dealing with the outside world.

To defray the torturing mental anguish, I would periodically place myself in wishful imaginative thinking: "I preferred to have been better off being an orphan, and never have known the true identity of my guardians." The majority of my existence has been this inner network of vagueness, and questionable identity. Even now, these domineering thought have never wavered. In truth, I have no parents, grandparents, or relatives.

For anyone to comprehend my plight, as an Asian American, **I endured many hardships in the United States.** It has not been easy for me to feel, or be accepted in this country. Honestly speaking, it is far more advantageous to be a Caucasian, and be readily received in many aspects of society. Please understand my adversity. **I am discriminated by my own mother, based solely on gender** (regardless of virtues or exemplary behaviors). **I was born in America,** however, I know in my heart people never truly acknowledged me, just on a superficial level. **Despite all this, I am proud to be an American, for the privileges/opportunities in this great country of ours, has given me the pride, nobility of acknowledging the awesome freedom, and advantages, that I sometimes take for granted. Amen!**

For evidence to pinpoint this: The priests and deacons I have encountered, with their comprehensive theological training/knowledge, **have failed to understand** the fundamental principles of respecting another human being. When unrighteous issues were brought up, these priests/deacons simply ignored my pleas, and sided with the wrongdoer, to appease their congregation. This revelation has allowed me to peer into the clergy's souls, their egos have clouded their clarity, and mission. I am not implying all priests are at fault, these situations occurred in a rural community. Clearly, the religious clerics need an in-depth study into race relations, particularly when mixed with marriage problems and conflicts.

I find this quite disturbing, we are all equal under God's creation, race has no face value. **It is your true heart, which determines who you really are.** Career wise, my husband is a physician (he is Board Certified). Yet, he has never obtained the higher salary positions, they are usually reserved for Caucasians (especially in New York), or relegated to specialists. **Then, there are those rude, stuck-up, and snobbish attending physicians. With their super-inflated egos,** who decides which doctor stays! And those to eliminate based on race, politics, and peculiarity. In our current nursing shortage, **I was black-listed from one hospital,** due to a legitimate complaint (over a salary dispute). I was unable to find another position, for that institution made certain to make my life miserable. Compounded with the fact, **I had no support system whatsoever,** except for my husband. I was cognizant of how fragile our lives were, being aware of not allowing society to set traps upon us. Yes, there are a plethora of scams. Envious individuals who for whatever reasons, ready to seize, and take advantage of you, with any opportunity, or on any occasions. **Case in point:** After the Beijing 2008 Summer Olympics, **my property was vandalized** (in a gated community, no less). No other criminal activity had occurred within our neighborhood, I was the exception. Again, this is a reminder where I stand in society. It is apparent to me, America is defined by race, for a select few. If someone dislikes you in any way, shape, or form, this is the outcome.

Through it all, my faith has never diminished. It is by the grace of God, I did not gravitate to the dark side, become a bitter or spiteful person. My story is a poignant one, since I was not fortunate to have loving parents, I have found my love for God. This is the lesson I have learned: **To strive to become a better human being.** With hindsight, the negative experiences has taught me a valuable insight, never blame myself, for the predicament I am in. If not for these difficult unfortunate circumstances, I am certain I would not be as compassionate, or understanding of others. A major turning point- you can only love another, when you love yourself first. I hated my reason for living. In actuality, it was a blessing in disguise. By the very fact, that life teaches every one of us to be accepting of ourselves and others. I deciphered not to hate those who treated me badly, instead I need to show more empathy towards them, this is the way to garner wisdom.

There is a saying: "Ignorance is bliss." **I would like to address the discrimination against gays, and lesbians.** Awakened beings know better. Such intent speaks volumes, about a person that harbors hatred for another person. You are literally damaging your soul with such wicked resentments. Please, maintain a forthright position. **The blessed spirit cannot fulfill it's promise to save you, even with an ounce of animosity.**

Follow the inner voice of wisdom (as it has done for me), to guide you to the intention of your journey- one of peace, and tranquility of knowing your true self, allowing passage to complete the destination. There are those who are resentful of their current circumstances. Unbeknownst to them, it is all determined by the actions of their past journeys. In addition, current ones to forecast the future.

Be mindful, we are <u>held accountable for every seed of thought.</u> This becomes our deciding factor within us, to alter our individual path, based on whatever valuable knowledge, wisdom bestows upon us. Truth be known, throughout the decades and history, what ails the human heart most profoundly is no love, or lack of love. Until one begins to unravel the mystery of this, there will be perpetual unrest in the soul for the quest.

The painful lessons I have acquired is, you cannot coerce someone to love you (in my case, my mother), it has to be unconditional, otherwise the end result becomes futile. **Genuine love, is the most sustainable and unbreakable bond, that can unite two spirits into one.** Defying the surmountable odds that comes before them (conflicts). Any form of love being seduced or bargained with, usually ends with drastic consequences. The ritualistic beings who utilizes love, to manipulate others to gain ahead in society, are plotting their downfall. Those elaborate plans ultimately backfires with eventual defeat, fatally misleading themselves.

Finally, love is a universal language that speaks to each and everyone of us, deep beneath our hearts and souls, regardless of race, status, or gender. Allowing us to grow, sharing life-long friendships, with the simple act, of getting along with one another. At the end of our spiritual road, we will be judged, and critiqued for our decisions, all leading to the final outcome. Nevertheless, **love is a major player in the cycle of life, consuming our desire to be cherished as a special person.**

In relation to love, the human heart can be quite fragile, summoning our vulnerable emotions to the surface, defying common sense, and judgment skills. In our weakest moments, it can lead to irrational discernments, and behaviors.

For this important reason, I advocate not to take advantage of anyone, especially surrounding the sensibility issues of love. **"Treat others as you want to be treated,"** is my motto. I am aghast, when someone uses me for personal gain. There is a feeling of immense emptiness within the soul, an impending setup of negative outlooks, including despondent episodes of depression, and inner-hate conflicts. Our immediate response is self-blame, with the rationalization of, how can I allow someone to do this to me? I must be a nitwit for this to happened.

To avoid this irreversible maze, convey those grieving sentiments to someone you trust, **do not harbor the poison within.** In the long-term, they can manifest gradually into sickness, or disease. It is vital to relinquish these psychological impacts through deep breathing, yoga, Qigong, meditation, exercise, and activities geared towards liberating the hurt, anger, and pain. Again, remain kind to yourself (avoid temptations- drugs, alcohol, etc.). **Do not yield to the demonic forces, which are capable of luring your feeble mind into self-destructive tendencies. Mentally block it out with: "Cancel."**

2) Nature

Everywhere you look, we are surrounded by the beautiful natural scenery of nature: Birds, flowers, trees, plants, mountains, the sky, all harmoniously existing with one another. Nature plays an integral part, in nourishing the mind/spirit/soul components of our human existence. It's serenity can channel the consciousness to connect with our soul, for it is yearning for wisdom, and intellectual advancement. You may be wondering, how can this be? Not obvious to the average person, **nature contains the essence of sustenance for the soul.** Only the spiritually advanced (true wisdom seekers), can harness it's vital resources of innumerable knowledge. And unlock the inner meanings within these immense landscapes. To widen their mental and spiritual capacity, towards deeper awakening of greater self-wisdom (**third eye-** between the eyebrows) attainment.

The extraordinary subconscious powers (natural elements) includes expansion of your sixth senses, clearing the route to read a person's thoughts.

To the general public, a tree is just a tree to them. However, the inexhaustible spiritual mind can gather additional wisdom from these vast forest terrains, which some have existed for hundreds, or thousands of years. **They hold valuable information** for the few, that can access their knowledge. In one's quest for the real reason, purpose, and meaning of life.

While I am in my garden, my psyche (mind) and spirit are in total synchrony with the earth. The quietude allows me to focus, and sharpen my mental preparedness for better clarity, furthering my true self in reflective-soul analysis, not solely spiritually, but in unison with the Universe as one. As the leaves are swaying back and forth in the wind, the adept can interpret their message, they are communicating.

During one summer, a black crow perched on my roof. He visited me at a predictable time. I was able to read his thoughts, as he was chirping. Later, through ESP (extra-sensory perception), I told him: "To go on with his life." He left, and returned periodically.

Nature is a refuge for the weary traveled souls. There is a saying: "Take time to smell the flowers." This is an important reminder to refresh our senses, the perceptible knowledge of ourselves. We are all works of progress. Self-awareness, is crucial to unraveling the inner functions of spontaneous cognizance (recognition), it propels us to evaluate what motivates the habits, thinking mechanisms within our intellectual brain, all necessary to make the critical decisions in our planning stages.

Nature has an **abundance of cosmic networks, intertwined with our space galaxy.** Even an unassuming piece of rock have valuable elements. It has absorbed light energy from the sun's rays with substance. Have you ever wondered why you feel revitalized following an outdoor activity? The reason being, we become energized from the mother earth we breathe. These natural assets readily feeds our soul, to rid the extraneous pollutants, which clouds those irrational reasons of uncertainty, hopelessness, and lack of faith within ourselves.

I find such comfort, and total peace from the outside world, all the while immersed with my shrubs. Try to dedicate valuable tranquil time alone with nature. **Feel it's essence engulfing your intuition, body, and being.** Absorbed the nutrients (sun), with each palpable movement you make. Become aware of your thought processes, along with the activity.

Attune the four senses (sight, smell, hearing, and touch) in synchrony with your movements. To become more adaptable, and receptive in receiving messages from the environment. There are informations zooming past us, in constant rapid motion (invisible to the naked eye). In order to retrieve this, it requires a milli-second in time to attain. Certainly, this is no easy task for the ordinary person. Mainly the pure hearted individuals can achieve this endeavor. Without a doubt, it is exceedingly unobtainable for the greedy soul to even attempt.

When you ultimately become unified with nature: The mental aspects of the psyche (mind) will naturally delve onto the philosophical plane, or realm of reasoning. To interpret these thoughts and actions, behavioral patterns, and instituting righteous motives, that dwells within us. **This collective memory phenomena, can instill the cause and effect mentality.** Preventing future unforeseen dilemmas, that may present itself in our paths. For example, by having foresight in advance, you minimize certain pitfalls, to pinpoint accurate decisions. Thus, avoiding repetitive mistakes. Once you enhance this concept to the next stage, these instantaneous intellectual processes, will allow you to master a multitude of strategies, and adapt to any perplexed situation.

Nature is an important aspect in fine-tuning our senses. And inducing the receptors in our brain, for greater comprehension of logic (locating sources of information from self). To distinguish the vital issues at hand, from the mundane, contemplate and assess the present reality of our circumstances, towards strategizing the actual realization of those dreams.

The multi-faceted entity of nature plays a remarkable role in negating the present distortions of unhealthy thought patterns. This permits the spiritual component to reflect back, stimulate the mind to immerse into your own zone. As if time has stopped, nothing seems to matter (no stress or worries). This can be the **pivotal point in time, where answers can suddenly appear unexpectedly, to underlying lingering questions.** Gradually, the natural tendency in trusting your sound judgment skills, becomes instincts to guide you against the conflicts, and struggles. Because life is so unpredictable, there are occasions when critical logical decisions, are crucial determinants to our fate.

Follow wisdom to evaluate your dreams, they hold vital clues to the subconscious level of unresolved concerns. Do not primarily rely on the support of others. Train in tandem with nature, to nurture your inner faith, and ability to deal with the complexities of society's issues. There is no harm, or wrong in asking for guidance. If the advice sounds convincing, it may not be the appropriate response. My suggestion is, trust in thyself. **Your wisdom contains unlimited knowledge power, and resources to all the questions.** Delve deep, the solutions are right in front of you, when you are able to seek it.

Many years ago, my husband felled prey to a pyramid scam (ponzi scheme). Along with a group of his friends in Qigong class. I trusted my instincts, and persuaded the person to return our money. Some time later, the unfortunate victims lost everything. The couple that perpetrated this crime, were punished to a lengthy prison sentence.

The lesson is: The true self can override any greedy delusions of grandeur, because the rational side will direct you into corrective reasoning ("If it's too good to be true, it usually is."), towards the main focus of truth.

In this world, there is no free ride, simple as that. To obtain anything in life, everyone has to earn it. From there, one acquires the virtues of integrity, and honesty in overcoming the enticements of immediate gratification. This is what maintains the soul whole, and intact, against the dark clouds of evil pollutants eager to invade.

3) Happiness

I have a confession to make. Most of my life I was not happy. Not until I reached my mid-fifties, did I finally grasp the exact meaning of happiness. Conveniently, I had ample reasons and excuses to be miserable, and depressed. Combined with the resilient skills of being a complainer, I based my rationales on a wretched childhood, lack of love or purpose ("Oh, what the use!"), and a poor outlook on life. These traits had a significant role in defining, and challenging my ability, to access any joy in daily existence.

Finding happiness, starts from within. I hated myself early on as a child. It became quite painstaking to even perceive, what the notion of being happy was. This is entirely a psychological process. Whatever the concept you place in your perception, becomes the outcome of one's thinking. For instance, if I set out to be despondent, the effect is a self-fulfilling prophecy.

<u>**FORTUNE COOKIE SAYS:*</u>

"There Is Only One Happiness In Life: To Love, And Be Loved."

Figuring how to become happy, is the first initial step. **Search for contentment in your existence,** be grateful for what you have (there's always someone worse than you), pay attention to your daily activities (enjoying every morsel of food), count blessings in disguise (good health, having doting parents, a loyal pet, etc.). **See beauty around you,** be appreciative of soul mates and significant others.

Discern what is vital, and meaningless regarding realistic expectations.

Have the awareness to look for creative ways, to enrich yourself with worthy causes (helping others, acts of kindness). It's our agenda to elevate our senses forward, invoking positive attributes to **internalize those feelings of real happiness.**

Let's face it, life is stressful, non-conducive to seeking quality of living. The daily rituals bombards us with unending distractions, aimed at throwing us off-course. To begin, there are no manual instructions to teach us how to be happy. A classic example, both of my parents were poor role models- sad, discontented souls. The appropriate measure is to select someone who is happy, whether a spouse, close friend, or relative. There are no shortage of alternatives, find your own niche. To me, **the logical reason for finding happiness,** <u>is having sanctity to offset</u>, and combat the on-going distress of every day life. There needs to be a happy medium within us, otherwise all else becomes off-balanced (the ying and yang). Leading to a course of chaos/turmoil into ill-health, poor choices, the dread of living, and total hopelessness.

Humans maneuver clever ways, to mask their individual suffering, with compensations of over-eating, shopping sprees, and addictive behaviors (drugs, alcohol, etc.). Once the cycle is over, this exacerbates their level of self-hating, and loathing towards increasing unhappiness. Definitely, not the way to go. These are all temporary quick fixes, intended to conceal the symptoms. **The short-term measures,** underscores the real underlying issues at hand. In effect, do not eliminate the root cause of the problem.

In a misguided attempt to deceive ourselves (including myself), it is habitually more convenient to escape with the dilemmas, rather than confront our fears. This is one characteristic of an unhappy individual. I can recall many instances, where I had intentionally made myself depressed, to prevent from exploring new adventures. By placing roadblocks of disappointments, how others will think of me, and impending failures.

From hindsight, I should have implanted seeds of positive attitudes, for a brighter outlook on life. **The other method is: Unravel the mental mess within your emotional state.** To determine, what precipitated the thought patterns of discontentment. To begin, **locate the source,** perhaps an incident, that drastically altered you to behave in the present.

<u>Our behaviors are comprised of past and present experiences.</u> Which directly, or indirectly affects our actions, and personal habits. The hidden agenda is- the more we delude ourselves, the worse the cycle of repetitive rituals becomes. There are no failures, except what we place in our minds. With every setback, do not accept defeat, keep trying, success is bound to happen.

In any given situation, we may feel weak and vulnerable. During this state of mind, **adopt a strong-will approach, to complete what you started.** This has often worked for me. Having a sense of accomplishment, no matter how trivial the task is, improves self-esteem, builds confidence, and conducive to gaining independence, and worthiness. During contemplative moments, I advise utilizing private time for self-analysis, insert happy notions into the inner core of your thinking, devise a goal to not allow the emotions to overtake you.

Allocate intentions of gladness into your being, it is not complicated at all. Be grateful of of your present circumstances, reflect on what makes you happy- your favorite food, a treasured possession, the important people in your life (spouse, children), a happy memory, and formulate in the mind to be glad to be alive.

ROADBLOCKS TO HAPPINESS:

1) **Discontentment-** Leads to continual unhappiness.
2) **Stress-** Can lead to ill-health, a shorter life.
3) **Greed/jealousy-** Leads to discontentment, misery.
4) **Hatred-** Leads to self-destruction, and bad karma.
5) **Narcissistic behaviors-** Leads to unending dissatisfaction.
6) **Comparing oneself to others who are better than you-** Leads to diminished self-worth/esteem, and jealous behaviors.
7) **Compulsive personalities-** Leads to a cycle of wanting more and more.
8) **Resentment/anger/bitterness-** Leads to spitefulness, poisoning one's soul.
9) **Hopelessness/low self-esteem-** Leads to suffering, a sense of emptiness, and lack of purpose in life.

10) **Ambition, power, wealth-** Leads to burdens of constant struggle, anxiety, and the unending quest to maintain it.
11) **Feeling sorry for yourself-** Leads to self-pity, and non-resolution of the problems.
12) **Regret-** Leads to repetitive self-blame, and greater negative thoughts.
13) **Negative thinking-** Leads to a self-fulfilling prophecy cycle of despair.
14) **Unresolved issues-** Is similar to a dagger to the heart, leads to a constant reminder of, should have or could have.
15) **Feelings of lacking love-** Leads to self-loathing.

Others maintain **a false perception of associating wealth with happiness.** In reality, this is usually not the case. **It is a misconception.** Survey any prosperous individual, he or she will emphatically testify it is far easier to earn the wealth, the strenuous objective is retaining the money. Closeby, are vultures on the prowl circling above, ready to seize the timing for a takeover, and take full advantage of them. There is the unending burden of outshining, or maintaining this lavish lifestyle amongst themselves (bigger yachts, larger homes, etc.), creating a plethora of emotional or financial strain.

Consider the fate of instant lottery millionaires. Who were ill-equipped, to deal with their sudden wealth, public acclaim, and notoriety. Prior to this, they led simple uncomplicated lives. Following the winnings, they were besieged by strangers, relatives, friends, all seeking to plunder their fortunes. A few have candidly revealed, the lottery became a curse to them. In the long-term, some were wrought with bankruptcy, destitute; worse off than they were prior to the riches.

According to Asian culture, affluence is personified and equated with status, having face (recognition), envy, and jealousy from others. **In childhood, I was instilled with the theory** to work diligently in life, to reap the rewards towards old age. The adage of wanting the children to become more prosperous than the previous generation, has never wavered from my mind, till this very day. The constant verbal reminders of their hardships and beginnings, all fostered an early conditioning, to endure difficult challenges. To reach a focused goal, of not letting our parents down. However, with the additional pressure of scholastic achievement, the happiness factor becomes compromised. Sometimes the best intentions can backfire. When children fail to meet the parent's expectations, they become sad and miserable adults. The stress can manifest into a lifetime of depression, anxiety, and enormous self-guilt. Therefore, I advocate to all parents, irregardless of race, **not to place the emphasis on achieving prosperity.**

One of the crucial aspects of awakening one's wisdom is: Which is a propensity towards greater happiness, without the added trappings, because of less burden within. **Letting go** of the extraneous nonsensical (nonsense) baggage, allows the human spirit to truly relish, and be grateful in every day life. To smell the air, realizing one is alive, to be able to control his or her own destiny, is a great tool for **inner spiritual empowerment.**

To value the real meaning of life: Is essential in the directive path, towards self-realization of higher spiritual quest, in search of enlightenment. I cannot emphasize this enough, we all have the full capability to be in control of our destiny. Foremost, the crux of the matter is, retaining the embodiment of total goodness as much as possible. <u>In the spirit world, re-negotiations are improbable.</u>

Everyone needs to execute an intervention, to promote more harmony into their own lives. Ask yourself: What is making you unhappy? Not satisfied with your job? Then change careers. Leave unhealthy relationships, take mini-vacations, modify poor habits, and **never allow anyone to control your life**. They will strip away your identity, and siphon the energy out of you. I say this sincerely from experience, because you are not living your life, it is their's instead.

There are alternatives to being happy, the choice is ours alone.
I have devised a happiness scale.

HAPPINESS SCALE:

- Put on a happy face- smile, and the world smiles back.

- Think of a happy thought (your favorite getaway).

- A chocolate a day keeps the sadness away **(yippee!).**

- See a hilarious movie, laugh till it hurts **(ooch, ouch!).**

- Go to the happiest place on earth- Disney World, your garden, or sanctuary.

- Perform acts of kindness, kind deeds warrant good rewards.

- Talk to your pets, they will nod and tail wag with everything you say **(ruff/meow).**

- Act childlike by yourself, without a care or worry in the world.

- Look at a favorite painting, pretend you are in it.

- Give your spouse a kiss, and hug every day **(smooch!).**

- Put plans into action, actions speak louder than words.

- Stop sulking, it will not solve anything.

- Very important: Learn to forgive.

- You can actually __________ someone with kindness, believe me, I tried it and it works!

- Stop the insanity, be good to yourself.

- Heck, if you can do it, so can I **(nah, nah, nah, nah).**

- Make a nice comment about others.

- When you are stuck in a rut, expedite an exit plan.

- Give someone an unexpected pleasant surprise **(surprise!!!).**

- So, what if you are not perfect, neither am I, join the club.

- Do not make fun of others, it will come back and bite you **(ouch!).**

- So, what if you don't like me, I like myself more **(ha!).**

- Do not be a sore loser, there are always second chances.

- Look, you do not have to buy everything you see, just think later on.

- Imitate the person who is annoying you.

- Say what, even when you understand them the first time around.

- Go ride a bike, ok you get the picture!

4) Meditation

Regarding our weekday lives, when the world is caving in on us- pressures at work, disorderly chaos in the home environment, relationship problems, financial burdens, unrealistic expectations, unforeseen circumstances, and the usual petty annoyances. They irritate our daily existence. Pertaining to these situations, it is prudent to not allow uneventful circumstances induce friction, and create unhealthy stress in our minds and sanity.

Humans have become lazy, relying on the advice of others! The source of powerful wisdom is in each, and everyone of us. Collaborate with yourself to transcend calm energy and say: "Cancel negative thoughts." Ingrain this ritualistic training for daily strength. This method is called: **"Wording way,"** whereby one's will can deliver results. **Embrace thyself to be a stealth warrior, and slay the psychological dragon demons.** To protect the three components: (1) Emotional, (2) spiritual and, (3) physical.

Utilize intellectual consciousness, take a minute, and **recite:** "Just a minor setback, I'll be alright." Console the soul with these words. Also known as antacid for an upset stomach.

Set aside a time, reflect on silence for awhile to soothe your agitated nerves. Take a short break, to unleash the inner angst within you. Do not use the usual ploy of, should have or could have mentality. These senseless psychological counter-attacks, are non-conducive to problem-solving. Instead, initiate mind relaxing techniques, such as deep breathing or meditation. This requires only a few minutes of your time. To promote peaceful tranquility, and eliminate the negativity, that can wreck havoc to one's mental and physical well-being.

Moderation in meditation is the key, avoid overdoing it. If meditation is misused, it can be harmful. On one occasion, a Master induced a highly meditative state on me. I became too focused with my concentration. Suddenly, I had no desire to come back to reality. I was fixated in the black darkness, drawing me to stay. Fortunately, there was an experienced person to awakened me back to the present. However, I believe meditation can be beneficial when performed appropriately.

There are reported instances in extreme cases, where some individuals have actually become mentally insane (unable to differentiate from reality), from intense meditation. They would meditate non-stop for hours without food or water, causing detrimental loss of blood flow to their circulation, from a prolonged posture state. These effects can be devastating, for it is irreversible.

Nevertheless, learn to focus and balance equilibrium of the mind, with the meditative process. **Free yourself from the burdens of life with emptiness** (remove all useless thoughts, by the complete visualization of spiritual wholeness, void of problematic entanglements-clear thinking).

5) Tai Chi

I recently took up Tai Chi lessons, and found it to be very relaxing and enjoyable. It is an ancient Chinese form of martial arts. **To enhance physical wellness, and cultivate mental alertness. In sharpening one's intellect, and to contribute mind/body connection, as we progressed into old age.**

The allure of the grace, and elegance of slow motion movements, is what attracted me to this exercise. Tai chi has the ability to increase bone density, promote blood circulation throughout the entire body, reducing stress, instill mental attunement, because the forms requires astute concentration. The most beneficial outcome, extending one's overall health towards greater longevity. There are countless testimonials in China, where Tai Chi Masters have a longer life expectancy, compared to the average person.

Furthermore, the **anti-aging advantage of Tai Chi,** far outweighs the debilitating state of our present health problems (obesity, diabetes, osteoporosis, Alzheimer's, etc.), the nation already faces. Another favorable factor, Tai Chi can be done anywhere and demands very little time, from fifteen to twenty minutes, at one's own convenience.

The ancient Chinese, developed this training **to enhance mental and physical body, while incorporating a meditative component** as well. It stimulates and forwards total well-being/healing, and balance of the ying-yang concept. When I am in my contemplative Tai Chi mode, I feel a great sense of calmness. Because the postures and forms necessitates deep concentration, along with **relaxation to create harmonious flow of chi (energy or life force),** from beginning to end. The movements are intertwined with simple and complex motions, which commands patience and perseverance to perfect those moves.

Those who are impatient and desire quick results, Tai Chi is not for them, this is a long-term commitment.

One of the wisdom abilities I can share, is the projection of my soul onto another dimension, accomplished within a nano-second rate. Performing Tai Chi (or Qigong) at the same time, while absorbing knowledge from the Universal source. For example, I can propagate (transmit) my being into space. **The secret, is** non-wishful thinking of any special gifts in return. The achievement of any insightful reception, requires an absolute natural state.

How did I arrive at this? My wisdom automatically guided me into this path. Consequently, I am able to reconnect whenever, without any side effects, completely safe, and sound. Another state **I like to project (my soul) into is the remote mountains in China, where surmountable wisdom are hidden, and stored in those cavernous caves.**

The accruement of this knowledge, are leaps and bounds beyond the ordinary, giving me the accessibility to foresee certain future events, that are yet to come. **The equation is: Pure heart plus pure mind equals significant holy knowledge, in the purpose to serve God, and fellow human beings.**

6) <u>Music</u>

Ah, music has the symphony of words. Which can transform the ordinary dulldrums of every day lives. Uplifting our spirits to another level of inspiration and depth of perception. The percussional instruments have this uncanny ability to evoke the emotions, even driving me to tears at times. Prompting myself to reflect at that moment in time, what I am feeling, and questioning my present state of mind. Music defies rhyme or reason, it taps into one's soul to contemplate our inner selves and feelings.

Music can relax our anxiety at the end of a very stressful day, thereby pacifying our senses to one of harmonious serenity. It can even raise your body rhythms, depending on the **tympanic beat,** <u>creating an entirely new manifestation of your outlook.</u> Either way, I have often found music to be a solace, and a friend for my weary soul. Best of all, music is never judgmental. **It speaks to my heart,** which nothing else can convey as deeply, and profoundly, in the innermost level of my being.

I can also **interpret and conceptualize** my mood, while listening to the wonderful inspiring sounds. With a peaceful tranquil effect, to offset the deep hurtful/painful times in my life. These rhythmic melodies somehow absorb the anguish, allows one to continue on their path, all the while reducing the burdening senses that dwells within our body. **In effect, providing a sanctum (sacred) of releasing negativity, and diverting our intuition towards another level, instead of consuming harmful emotions,** which are counterproductive for the soul.

Indeed, our souls all beat to a different drum. Go ahead, nurture your spirit with whatever songs that pleases you. **Embrace the sounds to flow into consciousness mode, incorporate the tone, and texture to find meaning within.**

Listen carefully, pay attention to the instruments (guitar, violin, piano, etc.). At the same time, insert your deep seeded problems and attempt to interpret, while grasping the music. Ask yourself to help unravel those complex emotions. Posture your body in a relaxing mood. The state of calmness in one's mentality, is conducive to the receptive channels within the brain. **To extrapolate those masked meanings or answers.**

We each know ourselves better than anyone else. It is therefore logical, the most reliable and resourceful way to resolve those complicated issues at hand. For example, why am I having this problem at the present?

Music allows one's soul to reflect back what had transpired to the current state. I find this exercise extremely practical. Without the expense of unnecessary, unsound advice of others. From my prior experiences, I wished I had listened to myself more, rather than receiving counsel from someone else, for it was totally incorrect. My motto is: **"Sound judgments comes from within, trust thyself."**

Again, penetrate into your mind, will it to provide the answers. In there, lies hidden solutions to your questions. Believe in yourself, that is what matters, formulate strategies with a backup plan. This I am certain- **your soul is eternally true to you, till the end.**

I HAVE MY FAVORITE MUSIC OPTIONS, LISTED IN ORDER:

1) **Enya** (I recommend: "The Memory of Trees" CD)

2) **Josh Groban In Concert** [2002] (Love all his CD's)

3) **Playlist:** The Very Best of **John Denver**

4) **Sarah Brightman**

5) **Celtic Woman** A New Journey

POEM

Reflections of The Soul

I came into the earthly world pure and white
    Imbedded in your body with all knowing sight

Infused with deep knowledge and worldly wisdom
    Waiting in time for you to release my freedom

To be reunited with mind, spirit connection
    Only to be distracted by your mindless actions

Yearning for my soul to be awakened
    So that your journey will not be forsaken

Along the way, my soul turned black
    All from your greed, nasty deeds, and bad acts

Only if you knew right from wrong
    Your life cycle would not have taken this long

Alas, you have sealed your fate
    All I can do now is wait

Hidden within you forever
    Hoping one day we will unite together

CHAPTER THREE

TAPPING INTO YOUR SPIRITUAL WISDOM

Dune: "The sleeper must awaken."

Here is a prelude to great wisdom skills- your soul can soar like the wind, with astounding awareness from infinity and beyond, in the fulfillment of far reaching exquisite holy attainment. That being said, is a lethal force against the dark Lord.

By this, **my soul have literally space-traveled to** the giant Buddha in China. It was an amazing natural phenomena on my part, to pay solemn respect. I cannot explain the reason for doing this, I simply knew instinctively.

I greeted Buddha with surpassed humbleness, expressing sadness for the suffering of the world, with genuine tears on my face. In heart, I understood implicitly the Buddha's words. He said: "Disciple, I have been waiting for you, you've arrived." His eminent bright golden light, was a presence to behold. Next, he placed the red circular symbol between my eyebrows. **Want proof?** I could never explain, or understood the slight indentation in that area, until now. I finally reached in this lifetime, to receive the monumental gesture, from Buddha himself. I asked for nothing. Reserved in my purity of heart is what I know. Then it was over.

Another treasured gift of wisdom- everyone possess a true spiritual age (no relevance to biological). To be able to derive this invaluable information, is from comprehending thyself. **I am four thousand years old.** It puts in perspective the pertinence of my mission, to the insightful provoking aspect/meaning of, wisdom-like knowledge.

Wisdom can protect you in times of dire straits, and prevent negative outcomes. However, you need to ascertain, and harness that power to your utmost advantage. **In order to proceed, there are certain absolute requisites** necessary, to begin this process. First, you must be genuinely compassionate in mind and spirit, to have any future progress or advancements. Do not be riddled with hatred, or spitefulness within your soul, otherwise all becomes futile. If your intentions are dishonest, you are merely deceiving yourself.

Having kindness, compassion, sympathy for others, are conducive, and essential to the correct path in searching for wisdom. **Promoting good deeds** from the inner core of your heart, without any encouragement or regret, is a positive step in the right direction. Why is this important? Because in absence of compassion, wisdom is unobtainable, simple as that. I am not suggesting you, to contribute large sums of money to your charity. No, it can be uncomplicated, such as random acts of kindness (aiding a total stranger in time of need, volunteering, etc.). Conduct this with willingness, effort, and determination.

In addition, the purer your soul, the easier for you to receive wisdom. Do not confuse wisdom with intelligence (having a high IQ) or book knowledge, there is no relationship between the two.

Needless to say, **if you harbor hatred,** or hurtful disparaging thoughts towards a certain race, person, or gender, all your feeble attempts becomes vain and useless. What you hope to achieve will not be attained. Animosity taints the very existence of your eternal soul, clouds the judgments or instincts within you. Therefore, blocking the clarity and passage, or path you desire to seek.

What is wisdom? The dictionary defines wisdom as: "Understanding of what is true, right, or lasting." My own interpretation of wisdom, is **your inner source guide.** Think of it as a compass, to lead you to the moral pathways, and directing you back when you are astrayed. One always need guidance, for there are precarious forces lurking about (greed, lust, ambition, jealousy), and tempts us unexpectedly, and suddenly beyond our anticipations.

Without wisdom, one becomes lost and trapped, in an eternal unending maze or ceaseless spiral, which ultimately seals our fate into a spider's web of undecisiveness, confusion, and the eventual manifestation of illnesses (cancer, heart disease, addiction, poor health).

To me, wisdom is a vital lifeline for my existence. It has saved me during countless times of crises, despair, inner turmoil, hurt, and life threatening situations. In addition, with advanced spirituality, you can ascertain foresights, altering the destiny and course, to your fullest advantage. This should not be taken lightly.

For some of us, **it requires many lifetimes to attain,** but well worth it. What I can tell you- wisdom in great depth will guard you, always be true, faithful till eternity and never fail, whatever the encounters. Furthermore, when you fully absorb the deeper levels and knowledge of wisdom, it can ultimately guide you towards the path of enlightenment or heaven. This source of intellectual awareness can thoroughly enhance your intuition, to avoid a cycle of mishaps or erroneous decisions.

The perceptive acuteness of your consciousness- enables you to extrapolate elemental circumstances in time, to prevent misfortunes from occurring in the future. For example, I believe events in our lives, repeat itself in cycles (relocating, career changes, etc.). You can apply this knowledge (from the past) to the current scenario, successfully avoid falling into similar circumstances, the second time around.

Life never prepares anyone for an impending disaster, it just does not happen. The greatest benefit of achieving wisdom, is the capability to have the insightful cognition of a backup plan, to execute when the need arises. The accumulated knowledge can also deepen, or **heighten other levels of awareness** (aura visualization ability, hearing, smell, and taste- prevent or detect food poisoning).

A common predicament most people have in today's society- is overeating. Once you have acquired an elevated sensory skill, you become spontaneously aware of your senses, in an auto-pilot state to cease when the situation arises. For instance, I eat two meals a day (most of my life) without breakfast, against medical guidelines. I have maintained a consistent weight all these years, without any diet regimens. Of course, the discipline is to maintain a healthy lifestyle, which includes regular exercise. This identical wisdom corresponds in preventing addictive traits.

The important facet wisdom provides, is total consciousness of one's surroundings. **This powerful knowledge is extremely valuable, which is infinite, and spans the space-time continuum (boundless).** It is immeasurable, of how far you can take this spellbound insight into the next dimension. With the enhanced vision of true clarity, steadfast importance in life, you can see: The total realization (the whole content), and mapping of your existence. Everything else is trivial. You totally get it, and grasp the picture.

I am behooved by some people (we are all human and make mistakes). They seem oblivious, void of any inclination, or clueless to their purpose in life. These individuals go through the rituals-going to mass, receive holy communion, and recite the prayers. On the contrary, their mannerisms, and behaviors have not improved (daily petty lies, lustful cheating, committing crime). Persons of this caliber are lost souls, lacking wisdom, or insight. They justify themselves by demonstrating trivial beneficial deeds, all the while conducting nasty old habits, as if nothing has transpired. I have news for them. **Unfortunate bad deeds omit the good deeds.** You are simply wasting your time in the circle of life.

Humans fail to comprehend the embodiment of cause and effect (or karma). The law of the Universe is exponentially fair, it does not discriminate. Direct actions dictate the future.
One of the frail traits of mankind, is jealousy towards one another. Once garnered with wisdom, moral superiority reigns, an instantaneous rationale to be happy and glad for them, not envy or harboring any bitterness, for they have earned it. Attempt to understand, the fruition are end results of accumulated positive karma.

There are many dimensions, in which you can utilize wisdom to your benefit. Again I need to remind everyone, in order to progress, you must acquire compassion, sympathy, and kindness in your heart. This is a necessary sequence, to initiate the chain of events that will enable you to succeed. **Profound wisdom delves into the deepest station of one's soul.** To awaken, and unravel mystical powers within us (we all have them). Altering each predicament in our favor.

<u>The exact rationale, is not be resentful of others,</u> when you can determine your own fate. This ability defies any logic, because it cannot be probed or examined, essentially extrinsic (not inherent) in comprehension. Subsequently, the wisdom you hold in your possession,

is a powerful tool or guiding light, to jump past the space-time continuum sequence of events, warning you in times of peril (a keen acuteness to prevent disaster). **The fundamental process- realizing how to salvage and protect your soul.** Similarly, **there are no coincidences in life, things happen for an instrumental purpose.** Most importantly, the possibilities are endless. This is a life-long quest. In order to be successful, become self-dependent, and not rely so much on others. My motto is: "Nothing is easy in life."

During your journey, remember there are distractions along the way. To test your endurance, and the ability to discern the true meaning, which you are seeking. Life always throws a curve ball, it is never stagnant. **Earth is another speck in the humongous (huge) Universe.**

Obtaining sharp perceptiveness, is quite empowering to your intellectual well-being. Your endeavors will have perspective, what you specifically want out of life, and interpret it's complex dialogue. At the same time, **<u>wisdom frees your mind, to master meticulous poignant tasks into multi-dimensional levels</u> (deriving two or multiple answers from the original one),** further expanding extensive knowledge source.

According to the guidelines of wisdom, it's magnitude are extremely resourceful and comprehensive. I have reaped the multitude of rewards, which has far exceeded my expectations. I never had any intentions of receiving such abilities, wisdom simply approached my inner being.

<u>By instinctual purpose,</u> I endorsed a devout spiritual training, coinciding with lengthy periods of extensive silence. Continuously in close proximity and synchrony with nature. I am most comfortable in that environment. I call this stage- **"awakening solitude," whereby I can by-pass the meditative practices.**

In my humblest humility, I have always considered myself an ordinary piece of dust on this earth. Unaware of this extraordinary power I hold (nothingness), the wisdom easily permeated into my inner thoughts. Best of all, **the inventions I am about to reveal, were entirely self-taught methodical reasonings, no mentors involved.**

GIFTS OF WISDOM

A) Communication With Other Souls

I can easily communicate with souls, either awake or asleep. With remarkable perceptive wisdom, **the eyes are the window to everyone's soul.** This is mastered from passing a culmination of tests, that God has given me during my lifetime. I understand succinctly to the precise point with every execution, when I penetrate into their eyes (or photographic memory). The messages are coherent since the souls are pure in their original state, and able to detect mines as well.

To determine I was not out of my senses, **I spoke to the soul** of my husband's Qigong Master. The revelation has to be very special, no one knows, except himself. I questioned this Master, that he possessed a clear protective barrier. Surprised, he concurred. He explained the enclosure keeps his emotions intact, and not permitting others to affect him.

B) Invoke The Invisibility Cloak (Shield)

Initially, I devised the protective shield to guard myself from evil forces. Later on, I decided to extend this benefit to others. **Case in point:** My mother-in-law **is ninety-four years old. I summoned an invisible shield on her behalf,** while intervening through God, via prayer. One day, she fell backwards (her entire body with full force) on concrete flooring. She sustained no fractures, or contusions. Only a laceration, with stitches. For her age and fragility, this is a remarkable testament to me. The phenomenal powers of God's intervention.

Two weeks prior to the BP gulf disaster, I had a vision of Bobby Jindal, the Louisiana Governor. I ignored the sign, and paid no attention. Then horrific tragedy unfolded- the implosive hyperactive gushing of oil into the ocean.

With news of tar remnants arriving on Florida shores, I became overly concerned, since I reside in this beautiful state. I could no longer bear the thoughts of in-coming hurricane season, and the detrimental impacts to Florida's economy.

Wholeheartedly, **I beseeched God to provide a barrier shield, entirely around the state of Florida. I then visualized in wisdom-eye formation, the appearance of an invisible protective armor against the elements.** With a sigh, I commented to my soul: "I hope all goes well from here on."

C) Foresight Enhancements

To retrieve foresight intuitiveness, is maintaining child-like mental attributes (pure heart status). With the guiding light presiding in me (rapid-speed procession), I have accurately predicted outcomes before they even happened.

Life is like a game of chess. I need to manipulate my move to prevent the opponent's strike. Asserting precautionary measures, I have to remain ahead. Seizing this knowledgeable gift at the most imminent degree, has proven to me time and time again, it works.

Back in 1997, my husband was in New York City, while I remained home in Upstate, New York (six hours away). One evening, I warned him to inspect his rental car, I had a bad feeling. He neglected my remarks, and returned home with the vehicle. The instant he arrived, we both discovered one of the wheel covers were stolened.

Case in point: Flashback to **when I was five years old.** At this age, children relate to the basic necessities- food and nurturing. Yes, I can vividly remembered, clear as today. Sternly asking myself at five: "When are my real parents coming to get me?" Throughout my life, I intermittently pondered over that remark, which did not make any sense then.

Wait, the plot climaxes! Around nine, **my mother professed a shocking revelation.** She recounted when I was a baby. One night, she left me all alone in the dark laundry basement (presumably in squalid condition). Her basis was the inability to cope, and control my incessant crying. Next morning, my mom realized the bottle's opening, was completely clogged. Due to her neglectful complacency, I was malnourished for twenty-four hours. Honestly, I did not absorb any emotional attachments, like a "dust in the wind." Strangers/acquaintances, repeatedly commented to my mom, and in my presence: "Is that your daughter, she does not resemble you?"

Forward to the present. My wisdom has alerted me, this incredible foresight premonition, existed back then as a young child. I had no inclinations, until reaching the **"awakening phase."** Those words are now coherent. They finally connect, and convey the significance for my future. And why did my mother revealed this story to me? Her conscience was rendered so touched by the sincerity of my soul (no bitterness).

I was in therapy for a number of years, to resolve my issues. The sessions seemed helpful, yet did not address the core of my real problems. Lastly, I deciphered the source (original cause), and the onion within me started to liberate. My pain, hurt, despair, rejection, one layer at a time. This modality (method) transformed the mental demons, towards the road to healing and recovery. The **multi-faceted approach (search, listen, and solve),** is applicable to many aspects of your life. Entering a new area of discovery into who you really are. Do you know your true thyself? That is for you to clarify, and answer.

If I had wisdom earlier, I could have saved myself from a great deal of frustration. I do not regret, for it has taken half a lifetime to solidify my skills. I am grateful. **The human soul is resilient, never give up on yourself!**

The spirit which resides in us, is our conscience to constantly alert us from right and wrong. Within it's **intricate labyrinth,** lies the source of considerable information accessible for retrieval and analysis. This motivation propels the psyche to re-examine, organize, prioritize it's true purpose. Towards the actualization of one's goals, and dreams. With the continual phase of purpose, comes advancements in receptive intervention.

The pitfalls that come along, are a necessary, and constant force of sequence and events that determines one's fate, whether good or bad. Be dependent on thyself, to extricate (release) the elements that unfolds your way. A reminder: The greatest lesson to be learned is- refrain from accepting hand outs, or advice from others. Then, you have truly earned your merit in the kingdom of God.

There is no harm in obtaining religious assistance from mentors, advisors, or parents, etc. From personal experience, their suggestions may not always be suitable for every situation. My view is: "Try to depend on yourself, wisdom is within you."

When do I know I've got it? The answers appear instantaneously in your mindset, eliminating any sense of hesitation or bewilderment. The amazing indispensable gift of wisdom- enables one to interpret beyond the usual analytical assessment, to whatever problems they may encounter. Once you seized this endowment, **one can intricately obtain an answer within another answer- to surpass knowledge, beyond one's mental ability.** The awakened mind, also broadens into another comprehensive dimension, encompassing greater spiritual, and intellectual reasoning (formulate definite answers).

When you achieve spiritual awareness, there are signs and signals around (to be realized), to provide clues in seeking the answers. They are there, you need to locate them. This is the difference between the believers and non-believers. Once the belief system is in place, the solutions will come readily, without any questionable doubt.

Bear in mind, wisdom cannot be accelerated in any shape or form. It is a deliberate, lengthy journey. As I have mentioned: **"Nothing is easy in life, it is not meant to be."** My useful advice to everyone: "When you desperately desire something in life, don't wish for it, otherwise you will never attain it." Irrespective of what you think, the way is, not trying too hard at all. You can undermine your abilities, give up, and fail. Buddha meditated under a tree for seven years, to reach enlightenment. One day, he understood it was all unnecessary.

There are common sense ways- to establish accessibility, in acquiring wisdom. **Contentment is a necessary ingredient to the equation.** Being discontent with material possessions, power, or status, impedes the fluidity of your course. As a result, becomes an obstacle crippling your ability to advance any further. Being content, frees our mind to the extraneous (irrelevant), nonsensical (nonsense) burdens within one's soul.

Tranquility and solitude, <u>has always been my superior ally to wisdom.</u> There is a saying:
"Silence is golden," is true in every sense of the word. I can decipher every complexity, and facet of receptive knowledge bestowed upon me, and assimilate (incorporate) it's deepest meaning. A disruptive setting, promotes stagnation of your thoughts, throwing you off-course to self-doubt, counterproductive behaviors (loss of faith), and the unending questioning of your convictions.

Try this exercise. While in a quiet state, ask your wisdom for guidance or whatever concerns you have. Speaking is unnecessary, silent communication is the appropriate method.
Answers do not descend immediately, they may arrive at a later point in time, when you least expect it. **Wisdom never fails, is inexplicable to rationalize how this works.** When it does happen, you will be amazed.

Prayer of any form has been an effective adjunct, towards my improvement in connecting with wisdom. Never underestimate the power of reverent petition to a deity. Unless you are an Atheist. Praying accelerates our bonding with God **(or True Source- the**

Creator), quelling (suppress) the doubts to distinguish what is real or false. Delineating the traps that comes along our every day life (avoiding scams, acute-reasoning, enhanced judgment skills). Knowing who your true friends and enemies are.

During times of vulnerability, ask him for direction, God works in mysterious ways. He is the one who can provide the sustenance of unlimited stupendous knowledge, in search for truth. My wisdom has never failed me, a constant companion throughout. Rest assured, you will be able to find serenity amongst the multitude of inner struggles. The key to unlocking the door: Trust and believing God is a force to make anything possible.

Why is wisdom so arduous to attain? Everyone's heart is pure when they entered this world, and circumstantially becomes flawed. Along the way, this heart becomes tainted, corrupted or badly influenced, either by our parents or egregious (very bad) choices. It is inevitable that each and everyone of us have to encounter instances of unpredictable experiences. Once the detrimental conditions affect an individual's mindset, it is intractable (difficult) to reverse the damage, which can lead to a downward spiral towards the dark side (hate, spitefulness, revenge, or destructive patterns).

One of human's frailty (failing) and flawed attribute, is the inability to forgive. The mind inadvertently sets up an irretrievable model of behavior towards getting even, an "eye for an eye" mentality. This monumental roadblock prohibits a mortal to truly forgive. **Forgiveness has a direct correlation with compassion.** One cannot be receptive to wisdom with deep seated feelings of ill-will towards another person, because it associates with the purity of one's heart. Can you forgive your enemies? You need to ask yourself this question.

The greatest assets of the human race are the ability to adapt, modify, or change their perceptions, and behaviors in life. Follow wisdom with this similar concept in mind. Anyone can reform. Imposing self-enforced internal dialogue, comes fruition. Certain situations arise to deepen our awareness. If you are able to master that source, you can recover valuable data from something trivial (source is your hindsight, which reminds you why things happen at an unexplainable point in time).

By this very example, you can fine-tune your ways of thinking. Analyze beneath the superficial meaning of one's existence, rather than utilizing irrational thoughts to sabotage your journey. Regardless, **be mindful- space-time continuum (boundless) is constantly shifting, testing your resourcefulness, will-power, and stamina.** Once a criterion is accomplished, the next level becomes more strenuous and challenging, in gaging your endurance to sequester the secrets of wisdom.

The **expansive wonderment of wisdom,** is the capacity to provide an individual superior ethereal (highly refined) qualities from mere mortals. I can attest to this awesome power. You receive an in-depth decisive perspectiveness, of how you want the actual outcome to be. Collaborating with self-reflection, inner wisdom can alter fate through your very actions into the next rebirth cycle.

Do not be misled by false misconceptions, or think for an instant, you can utilize this gift (wisdom) to defeat rivals, or for misguided intentions. Wisdom requires embodiment of mind and spirit towards good intent of self, and others only. **The objective is to save the most precious commodity- our souls,** and guide our families as well, in their journey to facilitate positive fortune/outcome for future generations to come.

The **concept of wisdom** is quite simple: "What is put forth, is the end result." There are two envisionings I would like to point out: First, "When you wish others well, you are essentially wishing yourself well." Second, Satan was originally an Angel, he abused his powers against God, and was banished to hell for all eternity. My take in all of this: "It is an endless battle to be a deeply religious person in this world, far easier to deviate from your true path."

AWAKENING YOUR WISDOM

There are two methods in awakening your wisdom: A) Contact a priest (exception- deacons are not qualified), rabbi or Buddhist monk, in your respective religion. Advise him to intervene on your behalf through God, to awaken your wisdom. In my case, my wisdom led me to a Buddhist temple. Unbeknownst to me at the time, was a "wisdom awakening ceremony."

B) Saying the words daily: "My wisdom has awakened," once or twice a day. To remind yourself each time, write a brief note, place it in a prominent place for recognition.

A monk stated: "Once you have attained wisdom, answers come easily." I concur. I have to acknowledge I would not be where I am today, without my wisdom. Just in awe and total gratitude. That appreciation encompasses contentment, happiness, sympathy and most vital, to love thyself.

By informing your wisdom to awaken, you are instructing (your soul) a straight forward directive to obey. This takes time. Do not expect miracles. The unexpected surfacing of subconscious cognizance (awareness), is the best surprise of all. Listen intently to your heart, accept the information to guide, and help you realize your meaningful purpose on this earth.

During the entire journey, **I did not have any advisors assist me in my spiritual achievements.** The lessons were hard-earned, grueling, and at times tested the strength and deepest core of my will-power, and perseverance to the maximum level. Honestly, I can take all the credit. With hindsight, I now comprehend **I did not want any handouts in life,** which has always been the real integrity that dwelled within me. This authentic wisdom acknowledgment has enabled me to endure the countless trials and tribulations, and exacerbating exams. While I remain unscathed in the process.

My story is a poignant (touching/emotional) one. Factually, **my mother** was a heavy smoker. **My father,** a chronic compulsive gambler, and a **deserter (he left when I was five).** Against all odds, I did not inherit any of their behaviors. Statistically, the chances are highly probable that children exhibit some kind of characteristics from their parents. In college, there were free pot being offered at the NYU (New York University) corner campus. I merely walked away without any hesitation. <u>What was my secret?</u> My wisdom and I made a clear concise choice. It is all about alternatives in life. The decisions you select, can have a direct consequence on the present and future.

Whatever drive that existed within, has also propelled me into becoming a better human being. My existence started to have meaning. **The more I examined the complexity of wisdom,** it's immense resources of knowledge, the greater sense of pureness I wanted to sustained. To be rid of the **evil contaminants** (greed, money, hostility, resentment). Further induced and motivated my ambition to reach my full potential, as a celestial being in complete unity with God.

Again, this book is totally dedicated to my beautiful and almighty God. Every human being has a spirit within them, with a resilient nature and strength. With God's connection in spirit, one can withstand temptations. Against the sinister forces that comes your way. **Face life's obstacles with an in-depth purpose.** Thus, enabling you to evaluate far beyond the present and it's significance, the rest is non-essential.

Another critical reason **why wisdom is exceptionally difficult to attain:** Satan is an evil presence who exerts his influence amongst all of us, ever-persistent in obtaining souls. The clever demon detects your weaknesses and takes full advantage of them, be it lust, fame, etc. Gather a steadfast spiritual approach, in resisting the lure of the dark side. Which is most crucial to have wisdom defend us, when we are vulnerable to it's seduction.

We all possess a backup source, it is our conscience that dictates, and warns us of devastating outcomes. However, when the enemy overtakes control, your conscience is dominated as well. No doubt, you become defenseless, and lack the willingness to resist. That explains a criminal interrogated after the offense. His response is: "I don't know why I did this."

<u>I perceive the lethal powers of the demonic forces.</u> For I have been tested above and beyond my abilities. I can say this. Your true salvation is with God, or whatever religious faith you subscribe to. Against the inevitable darkness that hovers over. To deny it, is simply lying to oneself. God embraces love and compassion, while evil condones spitefulness and retaliation (when the hate boils over, inside your heart). In simple terms, **I value wisdom as the warrior anti-virus for your software.**

Wisdom is ever-present, to safeguard your soul from the continuous onslaught, and invading sadistic seductions of the other dimension. Bear in mind, the diabolic purpose is to pollute your soul to the point of no return. With cloudy blockage in deterring you from navigating your true path. Harnessing wisdom, is becoming resourceful with self-knowledge in dealing with whatever comes your way, intuitively and logically. **The voice of logic takes precedence and pervade within your spirit, in the form of sound mind reasoning.** At my weakest point, I always ask God for support, and somehow my prayers are answered.

Coincidentally, blind-sightedness can submit to compulsive/ misguided indecisive decisions and judgments, which further complicates the mission. **In life, a disastrous repercussion reinvents your entire destiny.** Furthermore, those who continue a lifestyle of despicable acts, will forever sealed their own fate in never discovering wisdom. The soul becomes decayed, precisely what the devil wishes to accomplish. In terms of perpetual spirit, these unfortunate souls possess little conscience, or remorse for their actions (no emotions, expressionless features).

My grandmother passed away in her early-thirties during childbirth, long before I was conceived. I have no photographs of her either. One night, at age twelve, **I saw a vision of her in hell.** She appeared in a dream. Regarding disbelievers, maintain an open mind. Most succinctly, **hell exists.**

Over **thirty years later,** I visited a Buddhist nun director, and conveyed my story. Immediately, she understood perfectly and said: "Your grandma was attempting to reach you, to release her." Now, I do get it. Self-wisdom informed me. I was the only one capable of saving her. The nun made a special request for her salvation. I prayed to God. Love conquers all.

In 2009, my husband's father died. I have never met him. I was minding my own business, watching TV. All of a sudden, his voice telepathically came to me. Pleading me to notify his son and family to forgive him, so he can pass on. Why is this pertinent? He abandoned his wife/children a long time ago. **The overburdened soul is trapped in the nether world (purgatory).**

My father-in-law approached me. For what reason? I am the pure hearted spirit, who is receptive in receiving these messages from other dimensions. In other words, I am the connection to break their bondage. **An in-depth rationale:** Once deceased, the physical body diminishes into dust. Our souls remains. Too late to undo past deeds, it is all-knowing. Also known as insider trading in the under world.

For those contemplating to inflict harm unto others. I warn you. Be very afraid, do not deliberate on it. Do not give in! I am imploring you to reconsider other options. Concerning money, love, or marital affairs, this is not worth losing your soul. You are condemning your very existence, not the other person's. Whatever propels that inner hate, ask the True Source for guidance, and miracles do happen.

All those financial wizards being incarcerated. Would have unlikely committed their crimes, if they were aware a lengthy prison sentence awaited them, prior to their actions. Wisdom's defense is to secure protection against the pitfalls, that suddenly intrudes upon us.

One useful strategy I like to share in offsetting those angry feelings, is to trace back to the source of the problem, and dissect the issues that are causing you grief. It requires an analytical, fair, and objective mind. To evaluate the entire situation. Probe further, instead of jumping into conclusions. Ask yourself. Could the problem have been inflicted by me? What lead to this outcome, and how can I find a peaceful resolution to remedy the dilemma?

There are always tangible ways to avert disaster or escalation. Ventilating or writing a letter to explain my feelings has worked for me. When I reminisced about the past, I now realize how silly I reacted at the time.

By receiving wisdom, you can interpret the slightest notion, and extend that thought to decipher encyclopedic (an encyclopedia) codes. This is how great and **wonderful wisdom is- transforming you into an illuminating level of spirituality, directing one onto the path of light** (or righteous path).

One of the common trait of Saints- they are brutally honest and hold no judgments over others. In essence, they are perfect beings. My spirituality with God is of a true genuine nature. It is inherently clear, he has been continuously kind to me. These Saints are my idols, and role models. Inspiring me to become a better human being, for I am no way near their caliber.

It saddens me greatly when I see individuals straying from their path. Instead of reforming themselves, they utilize daily lame excuses for personal comfort. These beings become pathological liers, disregard other people's feelings, and lack remorse for their actions. I like to enlighten others. <u>This is how I practice wisdom to deal with deceitful characters.</u> We moved to a new gated community. Our Homeowner's Association required live oaks be planted on the property. I personally accompanied the landscaper to pre-select (tagged) the trees. On day of delivery, I knew instantly, one of the oak trees were switched. Not the one I had chosen originally (also from photographic memory). How did I dealt with the landscaper? In my heart, I was cognizant this man was dishonest, yet I deliberately remained silent. Would it have altered the outcome, if I confronted him with this information? Probably not. To the contrary, the opposite would happened. He will deny everything, and resent me for it.

Under these circumstances, wisdom guided me towards the **virtue of cautious self-introspection (self-examination).** The other person will unlikely modify his behavior. Even though I was deceived, in order to pass this intricate exam, with foresight dexterity, I showed compassion and forgave him. To take this experience further, life is not about winning or scoring points. As a matter of fact, the importance is continual disciplinary exemplified kindness, for everyone. **Manifesting a ripple-effect of delivering God's teachings, into productive humility and action.**

Back in 2000, **my mom enticed me with her greed.** In Chinese New Year tradition, it is customary for the parent to present their children red envelopes containing money ($100.00 was not shabby then). After she handed the envelope, a small argument ensued. My mother spitefully asked me to return the money. I returned the money immediately, without hesitation.

Many years following this incident, I look back not having the slightest regret. In my soul, I made the right decision. Majority of my life, I have never valued money. I have seen, how it has consumed my mother's soul. Because I was not easily tempted by greed, I passed the test, and she failed. Having the wonderful wisdom as my guide, I can now decisively interpret this incident. Assuming the person had no intentions to begin with. Why would I accept, when it was never meant to be?

This is **the inner core of my integrity and principle (the moral fiber of my character), which has propelled me to be what I am today.** No one in this world, including my own mom can buy my heart, with any monetary sum. A most valuable lesson I like to share- I eliminated the burden, which is one of the **deadly poisons** (greed) hindering one's path towards acquiring wisdom.

One of the basic **errors humans make during their lifetime-** their perpetual obsession on the here, and now. Rather the end result of one's visions. They blindly navigate minus the slightest inclinations into their actions, with the consequences of repetitive mistakes upon themselves. Flanked by wisdom, I have already devised a cohesive (devoted) fathomable plan to execute with minimal damage to my existing soul, in preparation for my exit strategy. I use this extensive knowledge to arrange for an improved fate, destiny, and future in the on-going cycle of life.

This is what the great religious minds and gurus have known all along. Some desire to immersed themselves with this precious insight for themselves. Instead, I want to share this secret, whereas others are hesitant to reveal.

The gate of heaven is not easily accessible. Despite the odds, with wisdom, one has the edge over mere mortals. We are forwarding the heavenly path where there is no fear of death, everlasting freedom from immense emotional burden, and our conscience is clear, with minimum trappings of guilt or remorse. On the opposite coin, those who follow a lifetime of deceit, lies, or evil, have incurred the fate for additional pain, suffering, and punishment.

Make no mistake, **exceptional wisdom is a lethal and powerful weapon to protect you infinitely.** Those lacking insight, will incessantly be envious of others who are wealthier, or better off than them. The accruement of fortune and success are derived from hard-earned efforts.

My emphasis is- we all need to work and improve ourselves, on a conscious level. Recognize the flaws (lying, cheating, etc.), and correct them. **Do not waste your valuable time pursuing worthless causes.** They are self-defeating prophecies, not conducive to your worthiness as a human being. It is yourself, you should be concentrating on. The basic principle can be as benign as working on your tardiness to reduce stress. Pursue interests that promotes happiness for thyself. Expand your inner world. You will become self-reliant and more confident. Why is this important? Achieving wisdom is contingent upon self-help, no reliance on others to reach that goal.

Finally, when you have acquired wisdom, the outcome is of undeniable exhilaration. The advanced spiritual mind increasingly sharpens it's clarity and dimension. **This includes intuition and powerful wisdom in unison, to resource hidden knowledge unbeknownst to man (a maze within another maze). The gateway to a unique realm of "supreme holy intelligence" awaits there.**

WORDS OF WISDOM

****

1) Trust in almighty God, he will never betray or let you down.

2) Trust wisdom, which is within you, to guide and lead you to your salvation.

3) Beware of some friends you have, for they could become your worst enemies.

4) Loneliness can be a great solitude- it reaches deep within your soul, to find solace and peace, which you wish to seek in life, and to finally validate your own purpose. That lonely place forces one to recognize, and acknowledge our faults and mistakes. To rehabilitate ourselves and discover answers to what is the true meaning of life.

5) True wisdom comes from not seeking advice out of others, rather when the answers are derived from within yourself.

6) When in your deepest darkest hour, where fear, hopelessness, or anger possesses you, reach out to God, the Universe. The response will come to you in unexpected ways.

7) Pain and suffering are part of life. The hardships, roadblocks, challenges, were all tests. To evaluate us and determine our destiny towards our next journey.

LIFE'S LESSONS LEARNED

1) Thank you for my poor humble beginnings:
   *** It has made me grateful, not taking things for granted, enabled me to be self-reliant/independent, and has helped me to stay grounded. Most of all, never forget where I came from, to what I have become today.

2) Thank you for giving me horrible parents:
   *** I know the true understanding of losing a loved one. What it really means- that you cannot get what you can never have, and not take my significant others for granted.

3) Thank you God, I love you:
   *** I am eternally thankful to be your humble servant. For you have shown me the light to save my soul, which led to the true meaning of life and this book.

4) Affliction with "Ovarian Cancer":
   *** I experienced the real essence of immeasurable pain and suffering. To truly value life, and view it as another journey. And treasure each day, as if it was my last.

5) Thank you for the racism:
   *** I will treat another human being with dignity, kindness, and respect. It has disciplined me to forgive, have compassion, especially those who have wronged me.

6) Thank you for the hatred:
   *** It has enlightened my wisdom and insight.

7) Thank you for the hurt:
   *** It has enabled me to heal my soul.

8) *** Respect people of all races, social class, that person may save your life one day.

9) *** There are no coincidences in life. Events happen to deepen our awareness and teach us lessons.

10) *** Without compassion, one cannot develop wisdom and spiritual attunement.

11) *** The trials and tribulations of my entire life, has been all a test. To determine the true integrity of my soul and worthiness as a human being.

12) *** When your heart is pure, you become invincible, for no one can hurt or corrupt you.

13) Searching answers from another:
    *** Listen carefully, he or she has revealed through unapparent spoken words.

14) Thank you for my soul mate:
    *** He has educated me to be patient and to compromise.

15) *** Life is a canvas, it is totally up to you with what you paint on it.

16) *** Do not take things for granted. For it is a blessing in disguise.

17) *** Happiness is when your true self, purity of mind, and soul connect. Knowing that no materialistic, monetary, or any unworthy value is necessary to satisfy you (contentment).

18) Deep spiritual awareness:
*** Enables you to advance to another higher level beyond your expectations, and can transform your being, which supersedes anything else in life, the greatest gift you can give to your soul.

19) *** Forgiveness is an extremely consuming test, for the intermittent memories are purpose-destine roadblocks to self-redemption.

20) Character virtue qualities:
*** Becomes apparent through thoughtful deeds, negating the necessity of compliments from others.

CHAPTER FOUR

FINDING YOUR SOUL MATE

Pride & Prejudice: "You have bewitched me body and soul, I love, I love, I love you."

First and foremost, the most crucial element to seeking your mate, is not judging on superficial features. Looks are so deceiving. We all eventually become old one day, you need more substance in a person, to truly sustain a relationship. By most accounts, people make a dire mistake and neglect to evaluate their in-laws, prior to marriage.

It is equally important **to select your mother-in-law,** for a disagreeable one can wreck your close union. Just think about it. They have acquired a lifetime of cunning mental maneuverings, and experiences that will surely challenge any bondship to it's core. I have observed enough in my life, irrelevant to race or ethnicity. In my honest opinion, I believe six out of ten mother-in-laws are difficult. For they have their own agendas, wishes, and desires.

Do not misunderstand, I am not implying all in-laws are terrible, you are most fortunate if you encounter a caring and loving one. On any given talk show today, there are marriages in the brink of disaster, because the mothers either interfered, or attempted to dominate the couple.

Being Asian, I particularly warn couples regarding mother-in-laws who are widowed. Frequently, they latch onto the son or daughter to suit their own conveniences. A common tradition in our culture- is to be respectful and honorable to our parents. Yet many times, they cross the line, burden you with their repetitive stories of a sad life of hardship, and loneliness.
This ingenious ploy makes you utterly guilt-ridden, and therefore bend to their wishes, at the same time neglecting your own needs.

Another oversight married couples erred on, is residing with the in-laws. My therapist once revealed to me: "There are high rates of suicides in China, amongst brides living with the husband's family." I am not surprised one bit. To make matters worse, the young wives oftened suffer in silence. A sad tragic plight, indeed.

There are exceptions of course. What if you found your soul mate, and wary about the in-law? Retain your mate. Subsequently, if someone has over-stepped his or her boundary, do not hold back your feelings. Ventilate and express your unhappy sentiments calmly towards that individual. Allowing the emotions to stagnate in your mind, will fester into anger, hate, and resentment for the other person.

The **second requisite is to distinguish a person with your heart.** See pass their physical being, examine their souls. This matter should not be taken lightly, since the individual will remain with you for a very long time. You can judge a person by their own actions, whether they exhibit any signs of honesty, humility, compassion, integrity, and self-worth. Yes, at times you need to test that prospective mate, by inquiring them with the same questions at different occasions, to evaluate the reply.

I totally disagree that opposites attracts. Once the sparks of passion and excitement starts to evaporate, you begin to visualize the eventual letdown of how little you have in common, after all. So vital to find someone with similar interests- schooling, hobbies, likes, and dislikes. I am a fan of the popular TV show: "HGTV." It is not surprising to see how couples resolve disagreements over living arrangements, home décor, and even color choices.

Make a wise decision- do your homework! When you go to a supermarket, you pick the best fruit possible. The same applies to searching for a mate. There are a myriad of choices, so why not select the one to suit your needs? It is trial and error, simple as that. Over time, you will gain the confidence to judge a person perceptually (by perception/intuition).

Third, most frequently **I see couples disputing over their finances.** Let's face it, we live in a world today where the emphasis is on status. Every magazine or TV commercial, seems to overwhelm us of the have and have nots (oh, Jesus!). I personally do not feel money should determine a mate. In my generation, money was not such an issue then.

Times have changed, I firmly believe the need to address this concern. Society nowadays have credit card debts, over-extended loans, car/mortgage payments, and compulsive shopping habits. Consistently on the news, are stories of marriages failing due to financial mismanagements, and poor decisions. The saddest part in all of this, they miss out on their love for one another. The overriding factor: Love sustains a marriage, and conquers all.

Thereby, when selecting a future mate, ask yourself honestly, are you comfortable with his or her finances? Question if you can weather the ups and downs of a marriage, when down the road that person succumbs to employment loss or health problems. **Bottom line: Be careful who you marry.**

You can wisely prepare yourself by choosing someone in a stable profession. Visualize yourself twenty or thirty years in the future with this individual, whether he or she can provide for your financial stability. The less stress in a marriage, the longer you can maintain it's longevity.

Fourth, the other essential and profound component in any relationship, is **honesty and trust.** By observation, couples who meet on first encounters, are too blind to see beyond the physical attractions. They are giddy to the point of ostentatiousness, impressing one another.

I have been there, and done that. My pet peeve is: I disagree with people who are pretentious. I describe them as: **"Phony baloney."**

When you are dishonest with yourself, how can you be honest with others? By deceiving themselves, lying so often, self-comprehension becomes inapparent. It is human nature to seek an attractive mate. I believe if one is blessed with beauty, it was bestowed by God.

Therefore, do not misuse that gift. While abusing your wiles (deceit) of seduction, others will ultimately see through you. Permeating a lasting impression on your true nature.

Building honest integrity is vital for one's connection. Without trust, love does not endure. Leaving a bitter taste to each other's soul. Establish this early on, if you really care about the person. **How do you facilitate trust?** First, be open, communicate with fairness. Followed by sincere moral conduct, treat others as you want to be treated, and ventilate those needs (emotional or otherwise). Most definitely, impressed the other to do the same. This corresponds to an amiable verbal contract essentially, cementing a bond that will anchor any turbulence. Testing the trials and tributes of any marriage or relationship.

The other **principal mutual agreement is financial trust.** These days, couples constantly argue over money, and lack of it. Ladies, if you are high maintenance, do not temporarily commit to someone with good looks, who cannot provide for you in the future. Know yourself. I have noticed women marry handsome men. Later, children are involved. By then, they are discouraged when the husbands earns low salaries.

Men, while searching for a mate, **be inquisitive about their spending habits.** I have witnessed cases, where women have bankrupt their spouses beyond the limits, with incessant shopping sprees. I am utterly dumbfounded, how a woman spends her (or husband's) money on a weekly manicure/pedicure, when it could be allocated to a trust fund for their children's education, or a rainy day.

Establish a financial plan. Prior to marriage, do not loan excessive money to your mate. This is a setup for disaster. Be aware of each other's expenditures, for you can prevent major arguments in the long-term.

I want to emphasize this very clearly, marriage is for lasting binding love. If anyone wishes to play the field and make reckless choices, please avoid matrimony. Not only are you damaging your soul, but imprinting a permanent scar on the other as well.

TIPS FOR MALES SEEKING A SOUL MATE

1) **Judge Her Inner Soul-**

It is natural for all of us to seek an attractive partner. Appearances are misleading. Ask thyself if this person is right for you, trust your wisdom, the answer will come from within.

2) **Find Common Ground-**

Inquire someone with similar interests and goals in life (faith, hobbies, travel).

3) **Know Thyself-**

Ask yourself sincerely, what you desire in a soul mate. If your expectations are exorbitant, most likely, the other party cannot measure up to them. Then, you are in for a real disappointment.

4) **Know Her Spending Habits-**

By this, I mean be aware of the high maintenance types. If you happen to see her with the latest "IT" handbag every week, manicured nails, processed hair, etc. Recognize they would continue with this lifestyle. They will drain you of your budget, and exhaust your income financially.

5) **Assess The Future-**

Can you see yourself with this partner for the next ten or twenty years? Do not obsess with the present. Look ahead in the distant.

6) Define Your Home base-

I see this pattern repeatedly. Couples constantly squabbling over household chores and duties. Guys, if you are the lackadaisical type, do not seek someone like yourself. Visit her home. Is she a clutter or hoarder? Are you a neat freak? These obvious traits do not mesh, and will definitely create havoc in a relationship.

7) Be Analytical-

Every woman likes an intelligent man. Ask her questions regarding the future, this will peak her interest towards you. Not only that, you will gain some perception into her expectant hopes.

8) Do Not Be A Miser-

This pertains to the early stages of dating. If you really like this mate, by all means, avoid being a cheapskate. Girls are turned off by this, and probably will not give you a second chance.

9) Be Sincere-

By bestowing trust and honesty towards another human being, the Universe can only grant you good tidings. A woman's emotion is not to be trifled with. She will remember the slightest insignificance, with utmost clarity of that particular time, place, or event. In showing her your genuine affection, you have captured her heart with an everlasting impression.

10) Be Successful-

What most women want in life is to have emotional/financial security and provisions for their children. They prefer a man who takes responsibility. Nothing attracts a woman more, when they see a successful man. So, work hard, build your career with a good portfolio. They will come to seek you out. One caveat: Beware of gold diggers!

11) Test Her-

After a few months of dating, offer your mate a fifty or one hundred dollar bill. When she accepts, it is a red flag. This is an honesty test to decipher her true character, whether she is materialistic or needy. Her ethics and overall integrity. Question: Does she love you or your money? This is the deciding factor.

TIPS FOR FEMALES SEEKING A SOUL MATE

1) **Judge His Inner Soul-**

The eyes are visions into a soul. I surmise women are biologically more perceptive than men, perhaps by being observant. Ladies, look into his eyes when he speaks. Your inner wisdom will guide you.

2) **Be Natural-**

We are constantly bombarded by televised ads, and trends of what beauty is. Women in general have fallen prey. By obtaining the latest botox, breast enhancements, hair and nail extensions, etc. Honestly, I believe men prefer someone original. Unaltered, and not having to stare at those bowling balls protruding from a woman's chest. Eventually, the modifications fade. Where is the real substance, and how do you sustain a relationship?

3) **Devise A Plan-**

Ask yourself, what do I request in a man? Is it love, comfort, or financial stability? Do not allow emotions to cloud your judgments. The irreversible pendulum of choices rendered, defines the next chapter.

4) **Do Not Look In The Wrong Places-**

Once you have devised a plan, do not deviate. You simply cannot find a lasting courtship from roaming the night clubs, bars, or newspaper ads. Do your homework. Attend stable circles (church groups, club activities, etc.).

5) **Know Thyself-**

It is noteworthy to assess your own needs, prior to selecting a mate. Are you high maintenance? Do not choose someone who cannot support your habits in the future. Once the answers are found, you have mentally provided yourself a safety net, of weeding out the undesirables.

6) **Assess The Future-**

How you select a mate, affects your entire life. Be strategic, formulate a prepared plan. Choose a partner with a steady career, void of constantly struggling with relocating, and lay offs. Do not hesitate to ask him: "Will you love me when I am fifty pounds overweight, after I have your children?" If he second guesses, there is your answer.

7) **Do Not Sell Yourself Short-**

Frequently in magazines and real life, women sleep with a total stranger on their first encounters. How can you expect others to respect you, when you do not respect yourself? When a woman utilizes the art of seduction, there is no guarantee of a permanent relationship. Because a good man is asking himself: "If she can sleep with me so recklessly, how many other men has she slept with?" Therefore, keep your integrity intact. If he pressures you, refuse him, for you have weeded out the bad egg.

8) **Know His True Character-**

Locating Mr. Right is not a feasible task in itself. You have competition from other females, vying for the same man. Do not despair, my motto is: "If it was not meant to be, it is not meant to be." I believe fate plays a role. You may come across your soul mate in the most unexpected circumstances, an introduction from a family member, or friend.

My major criteria in discovering one's character, is through his deeds and actions. An example- does he respect his mother? Does he gaze at other females in your presence?

Be aware of very handsome guys. Other rival female piranhas are also attempting to seize him. Some are consumed with their vanity. Physical qualities can actually throw you off-course. Since it is difficult to truly consider the important issues of one's character.

I do not mean to be cruel and negative towards attractive men. A reminder: "Beauty is a gift from God." Ask yourself: "Can I hold onto him long-term?" For you need to hone your skills as a woman, to elude the inevitable traps of life. To exemplify, do not hire a young pretty baby sitter, avoid leaving him alone at social parties, be proactive in his business circles and friends, etc.

I am not advocating smothering your partner to the point of being controlling. No, when you involve yourself in his world, he will feel a sense of camaraderie and trust, that can evolve into a lasting companionship.

9) Dress Like A Lady-

I am repulsed, at how young woman carry on and dress themselves. You cannot command respect when you are not adorned properly. These days, I am shocked to see females behaving in the most un-ladylike manners, displaying their atrocious demeanors.

These same class of women wonder why they are not attracting suitable mates. The moral: You elicit unfavorable cads by wearing revealing clothing. On the other hand, when you dress like a lady, males will treat you differently.

At the end of the day, what a man really insists upon- is a loyal, affectionate woman without the false pretenses, who can cook a decent meal, maintain a family, and organize a home. To be there for him, and listen when he has had a bad day.

A man does not desire a woman with the full make-up, wearing the latest trends, etc. They simply need someone down to earth. As soon as the masquerade is over, he will lose interest in you. I hear repeatedly: "Good men are hard to find." Ladies, they are out there.

10) Find Commonality-

It is preferable to have similar tastes. If he happens to be a die-hard sports fanatic, you will subject yourself to resentment and regret. One of the overwhelming mistakes in couples, is the false belief or attempt to change one another. Usually, the results are very disappointing.

11) Avoid Addictive Traits-

Men who have compulsive personalities, such as gambling, drugs, or alcohol can be a liability. You may become drawn to their chronic habits as well. These types can be very charismatic and charming at first. However, do not be fooled or misled. The addiction phase systematically becomes overbearing. They often manifest into fits of control, anger, and hostility towards others, if anyone interferes.

12) Do Not Toy With Him-

One of the gravest oversights a woman make- is dating perhaps two or three men at the same time. Guys have feelings too. Once they discovered you are taking advantage of them, your reputation will suffer. Adversely, you cannot fully comprehend their psyche, the mental signals become unmatched. In essence, self-deception is inevitable. Apply careful consideration for others, karma is involved.

UNIVERSAL COUPLE ARGUMENT & RESOLUTION

****

ACT I: Spicy Tom and Saucey Susan are having a heated disagreement on ingredients. Tom is so upset, he is about to boil over. "Now, now, just simmer down before you get too acidic," says Susan.

Easy for you to say replies Tom, "You are bland as can be. Sometimes, you seem to shut me out. I plain had enough of this chewing back and forth, it is not going anywhere."

ACT II: After brewing about it, Susan finally says: "You're right, we need to put a lid on this, before we both become pasty and saturated." Tom, in his fruitful smile, agreed. "Funny, how we can go peanuts over such silly condiments, parsleys, and veggies."

ACT III: Susan churns in: "Oh Tom, you are so yummy and delicious! We were always meant for each other, in fact I am nuts about you." Suddenly, a blissful fruity tooty moment came to them. I know what, says both: "We have to compromise." From now on, they decided to discuss everything ahead of time.

ACT IV: They envisioned a sugary peppermint, spicy concoction of their favorite ingredients, all mix nicely together.

With their successful mixture and blend of delightful seasonings, it was time to relish the Splenda aroma! Spicy Tom then said: "I feel cool as a cucumber." With that thought, Saucey Susan says: "Let's get out of here in our escargot!"

ENDING: **From that Prego moment, their days became a Sunny D & Snapple delight!**

CHAPTER FIVE

SUSTAINING A MARRIAGE/ RELATIONSHIP

My Fair Lady:
"Why can't a woman be more like a man?"

One of life's most perplex (confusing) challenges, is maintaining a marriage. We all know that. When it could not be more complicated or stressful, children and in-laws are merged into the combination. **Matrimony is wonderful** when conditions work out, but undoubtedly horrific when the union fails. Consequently, this is a serious matter not to be taken lightly.

My father abandoned my mother when I was five years old, that devastated me. They both made terrible choices. She married him for the sole purpose of coming to America. My dad never loved her. I suffered the torment of lacking a stable family structure. Their misfortune cost me a great deal of mental anguish throughout my life.

Case in point: As a youngster, I should not have suffered what I had experienced. I was nine. My father stormed into the room, demanding money to repay his gambling debts. My mother vehemently refused. He resided elsewhere. At that instant, he snatched a large meat cleaver, in ready position to dismember her head.

Yes, **little Mae came to the rescue.** I was a scrawny kid then. Fear was not option. Concern for my own safety did not exist. Meanwhile, my brother was whimpering in a nearby corner. I have no other siblings. This was a **David and Goliath** (make or break) **moment.** I chased after my father and interceded. And saw the palpable rage in his eyes. He stopped, as I pleaded with all my might. Positively, an extremely emotional, intense drama.

There were other instances when Police were summoned at the scene. Each session, I had to intervene and diffuse their explosive, and charged arguments. My brother was nowhere to be found, he was hiding in a separate quarter. In due course, the officers became fed up. They only trusted my words.

From that day forth, I was my father's number one enemy. To rectify two adult's incompetence and immaturity, is a burdensome responsibility for a nine year old. In upholding my righteous fortitude, I sustained his verbal intimidating insults ("You are no good!").

I was not fazed by his hatred, the intense **love for my mother** superseded above everything else. In fact, I would gladly die for her, and not hesitate in a heartbeat. **This love is astronomical and profound- akin to moving a mountain with my bare hands.**

During my later years, I forgave my father. This was a monumental piece of the puzzle, in entering the steps, and mighty fortress of God's holy kingdom.

In other words. As a proponent of compassion, this single-minded action, had to have awakened God, or the Angels in heaven. **Giving up oneself for another (my mom), is an earth-shattering atonement for the sins of my parents.** God, I love you for this insightful lesson!

From an early age, I promised myself to make critical sound decisions, and avoid the irrevocable mistakes my parents made. I knew statistically the odds were against me. Since it is documented that children of ruined marriages, do not fare entirely well in their own relationships.

Nevertheless, I am a living testament of proving them wrong, my marriage has endured. In order to accomplish success, an enormous amount of complex, provoking decisions went into it.

I have ascertained observations in my lifetime. To assess why some relationships succeed while others dissolve. **The major mishap in failures- they select the wrong soul mates.** The second reason- not envisioning the long-term commitment, which they are about to enter.

The decisive crux of the equation to marriage is: **Do you know the meaning of true love?** I do. True love for me goes beyond the physical aspects. It encompasses a kind of affection that is genuine, devout, and unconditional. When that bond becomes so connected, you could complete each other's sentences, read their thoughts, and know what they are feeling at times.

The longer you are married, your spouse becomes an inseparable soul mate, confidant, and friend. Trust evokes a fulfilling reward for both, far beyond description. The love I am detailing is irrespective of status and wealth, whereas destiny can change.

Being affected as a child, without the love from my parents, no one can truly comprehend the depth and magnitude of that innermost feeling, when you have actually lost it. Nowadays, people have lost their sense of integrity, the real essence of love over the importance of money, status, and pretentiousness. Sadly enough, society's values of wedlock has diminished, the end result is mistrust, dishonesty, and betrayal.

One commonality of successful bonds, is that **they all compromise.** A rule of thumb I live by- I make an effort not to take advantage of my spouse. **I play fair.** Meaning, we engage as equal partners to navigate through the tribulations of questionable circumstances. Believe me! Marriage is hard work, one of the most grueling ordeals in my life. Like anything else, only the strong can survive. What you gain from a successful partnership is a sense of well-being, accomplishment, and pride. Compatible partners also create a happier and healthier outlook on life. Don't get me wrong. We all have our good and bad days as well.

An insight I have garnered throughout my marriage, is not giving up on one another. This is so vital for any relationship. It is easy to leave and walk out the door. Not a miscalculation I allowed myself. For I have failed in defeating myself by choosing a simple exit, just as my parents did.

Faith is an additional driving force in a bond. Once you relinquish another human being, the partner is left with a sense of emptiness, and despair. Of course, there are exceptions to the rule which dictates you to leave a marriage. When the individual is an apparent danger or threat, to violate your entire being (abusive, aggressive, or violent). For this reason, **I caution everyone to choose their soul mates wisely.**

One pertinent issue I like to discuss is to argue fairly. We all have disagreements in life, which happens to be the most trivial and insignificant. Each time, we behave more like children, and not as adults. After it is over, have you ever wondered how ridiculous the argument was? I have found a tried and true method: I take time out. I merely walk away from the situation, to settle down. You cannot fight fire with fire. One lesson I have learned from my past experiences, is never drive when I am angry or upset. Because the focus of attention is elsewhere, not on the road.

Furthermore, there are assertions **why the partnership fails.** Evidently, when either one or both partners becomes selfish, think only of their needs and feelings. The sad outcome of this emotion, can suffocate the love that needs to be sustained in any relationship. There is no give and take. It becomes too overbearing, and eventually the marriage falls apart.

Another major factor is when **couples hold grudges,** and cannot forgive each other. Resembling a disease, these sentiments can manifest itself into bouts of anger, hostility, and spitefulness. In turn, these hurtful feelings can last a lifetime. Quite devastating to the human soul. A reminder- problems worsens when children are involved.

The downfalls of doomed marriages are **infidelity.** To me, being unfaithful is the worst kind of stab in your heart betrayal, you can bestow upon another. There is no excuse for this behavior. It behooves me why couples marry in the first place. I cannot comprehend their frame of thinking. Why bother to deceive yourself into matrimony, and cheat on your significant other? People with wandering hearts should not contemplate being married, they are never satisfied, or grateful with their partners. The immense hurt felt by this union, can be irreparable to the human heart.

The other illusion is both mates attempting to change one another. The success rate is low. The reasoning- an individual's personality or trait is imprinted in adulthood, and thereby reluctant to alter one's behavior. There is a common phrase: "They are so set in their ways." As a result, the divorce rate has skyrocketed. Humans have never learned from their foibles. Fittingly, they have become accustomed to condoning the same weaknesses, over and over again.

As a chronic deception, repeated attempts at marriage emerges. All along, the root of the problem is within themselves. In effect, they impose demands, values, and wishes onto the other person. Only to be disappointed again in their mission.

One of the **misconceptions of marriage-** we visualize a Cinderella story ending, of happily ever after. Fundamentally, in real life this does not happen. Involved are two different personalities meshed together. Sometimes those conflict of interests or opinions clash, which causes soul mates to drift apart.

In essence, **marriage partakes** an enormous amount of time, patience, and compassion, for the relationship to succeed. Let's admit it, we live in a highly stressful world today. The gist of dilemmas evolve, when mates do not discuss their issues together. They ignore the disarrays, which are on-going. These days, people's lives are so intertwined with work, they seldom dine as a family unit. We need to change, to pursue precious quality time for ourselves, and significant others. I remembered a saying: "A family that eats together, stays together."

****

****

FORMULA FOR MARRIAGE

****

I have invented a simple formula for a happy marriage. Mind you, this is not a cure-all. Each successful marriage requires a collaboration of mutual understanding, endurance, and acceptance. The beautiful outcome consists of collective minds, growing and learning from those experiences, to share, and cherish the rare quality *moments.*

FORMULA

A + C + F + L + T = H (HAPPY MARRIAGE)

A- AFFECTION

C- COMPROMISE

F- FORGIVENESS

L- LOYALTY

T- TEAMWORK

****

****

INGREDIENTS FOR A SUCCESSFUL MARRIAGE

1) **Establish trust-**

This should be initiated near the beginning of a relationship. Trust is imperative in a union, just as a foundation is to a home. How do you create trust? By words, honesty, actions, and deeds.

2) **Share trust in money-**

Relevant in every partnership. One of the major sources of disputes is over money. Money is a complicated issue in itself, let alone when there are differences in beliefs between two people. One of the ways to resolve this conundrum (problem): Simplify your finances by:

*** **Remove the unnecessary cards-**

I prefer those gas credit cards which offer cash rebates. We use these cards for all our purchases. Towards the end, are cash rewards.

*** **Live within your means-**

According to the average household, most consumers carry a debt of eight thousand dollars, or more. The result of foolish spending and ill-thinking on their part. Not only is this unhealthy for a marriage, it creates further friction between the two. Spend wisely, carefully, and pay off your credit card bills at the end of each month.

*** **Be truthful-**

I know there are wives out there, myself included, who have gone out shopping, come home and stashed everything out of sight, from their husbands. I no longer commit this, I have reformed. I did concealed my acquisitions early in our marriage, for fear of his remarks.

My method of managing trust in money- by always leaving purchase receipts for my husband to view. This way, I can allocate the expenditures within my means. Reciprocally, my spouse can acquire trust and peace of mind, affirming the amount I have spent. As for me, trust is earned the honest way, not by deceptive means.

I am aware of two couples, whose wives have bankrupted their physician husbands, due to their uncontrollable shopping binges. Hence, present those transaction stubs to your significant others. He may not respond favorably regarding the outcome. With this technique, the trust factor is in place.

*** **Keep a financial journal-**

I have always maintained a record of my daily purchases. Again and again, this has been an invaluable time saver. With each monthly credit card statement arrival, I can easily detect any monetary discrepancies. By locating my diary, no guesswork is involved.

*** **Clip coupons-**

Due to humble beginnings, I am drawn to saving money. Coupons are similar to cash. I get tickle pink, when I attain the five-dollar ones, used in conjunction with sale items. Once the savings are totaled in a year, the amount can be substantial. By exhibiting trust (saving money) to your partner, he or she will value the contributing effort in the marriage. Including a sense of self-worth.

3) **Forgive one another/Do not hold grudges-**

I have stressed this before, so vital. It is a test for any marriage. If you can forgive your spouse, you are half way there. In addition, holding a grudge does not benefit anyone, only adds fuel to the fire.

4) **Do not get mad, write it down-**

I have found the most logical and sensible approach in dealing with my pent-up emotions. Avoiding an argument is advantageous for both parties. Whenever I become frustrated, I write my hubby a note explaining my feelings. By reason, I am not the type of person who pents everything inside. Accordingly, this is a healthy outlet to ventilate those sensibilities. Thereby preventing a direct face-to-face confrontation, which can lead to a major disagreement.

There are two requisites I am adamant about. The letters I write are truthful, not fabricated. Those written words can return to haunt me. Secondly, I always advise my husband to shred them afterwards for closure. This process has worked for us. After reading, he gains a deeper understanding of my true sensitivities.

5) **Saying: "I am sorry"-**

Now and then, it is inevitable to have an argument or conflict. Tempers can flare up and escalate to a higher level. Much easier said than done. How do you diffuse a situation like that? Even when my spouse is wrong and I am right, I say: "I am sorry," to appease him and end the dispute. Later on, I wait for an opportunity to correct him. Base your reasons on logic and clarity, for him to accept the rationale. Otherwise, it becomes baseless and you are the fool. Try it, this is effective every time.

6) **Ventilate your feelings-**

One of the things I do not like about my culture- my parents never communicated their feelings to one another. They built a barrier wall of bitter resentment and hostility. This is not going to happen in my marriage, I made certain of it. If something irritates me, I ventilate to my spouse at that moment, not days, or weeks later. This has attributed to resolving a majority of our grievances early on, and creating a more harmonious one.

7) **Pray for one another-**

There is a philosophy I live by- life holds no guarantees. As a physician, my husband has a very stressful career. He sometimes encounters life and death situations daily. I pray for him and believe in my faith immensely.

By demonstrating devout affection for another human being, the Universe cannot deny your intentions. Rather be honored by it. A sincere prayer in caring for others is a virtuous act. The heart is a powerful entity, it wills God to respond, and grant wishes. The act in itself is a true trait of compassion and selfless love.

8) **Do not take each other for granted-**

Out of every marriage, after a certain period, couples often take each other for granted. It is human nature. In our daily consuming lives, we tend to forget how important this is. One way I show my gratitude is by saying: "I love you." It conveys you appreciate him for who he is.

9) **Write notes to one another-**

I am not particularly fond of texting or e-mails. They lack the warm personal touch, necessary to communicate distinct heart-felt intentions. Personally, I prefer to write a note describing my feelings. The receiving end can value the fact you have takened the time and effort to compose those emotions. Ah, a Hallmark moment. I write thank you notes for the simple tasks my spouse has done. He may not say anything. In his heart, he knows I appreciate him. Positive reinforcements are an effective tool to rekindling the spark in a relationship.

10) **Go out of your way once in a while-**

I can think of no other reason to show greater affection, than to perform a special gesture for someone. It does not have to be expensive or extravagant. These exceptional validations will go a long way in solidifying your bonding, all etched in their memory.

11) **Hug each other-**

I have implemented this in the beginning of my marriage. My motto is: "A hug a day keeps the sickness away." I realized the simple act of embracing- is an acknowledgment of our souls as one. Fortuitously, creating a nurturing affinity between two spirits.

12) **Make dates-**

Worthwhile quality time is equal in value to combining sense of mutual purpose. Additionally, this is the period to have fun, laugh, and enjoy life with each other's company. That's what living is about.

13) **Try to eat together every day-**

I was brought up with this cultural custom. Most definitely, a good one. With increasing dual income families, it is a sad loss for everyone to miss out on family togetherness. A sense of belonging is lost. I firmly believe this tradition should be preserved, passed on from generation to generation.

14) **Exercise together-**

What could be more fun than physical fitness, enjoying the camaraderie, and encouraging each other to stay healthy? I cannot think of any activity besides this. Statistically, women outlive men in society. I feel it is incumbent upon the wives to support their husbands, in living a consistent proactive regimen. If they do not wish to become early widows in life. In direct relation to sedentary lifestyles and modern conveniences, we have become accustomed to a laid-back attitude. According to Kurt Vonnegut: "The secret to success in any human endeavor is total concentration." The purpose of marriage is having a life-long partner. The means of achieving and accomplishing this goal is through healthy living.

CHAPTER SIX

TEACH YOUR CHILDREN WELL

Willy Wonka & The Chocolate Factory: "So shy it is a good deed in a weary world."

Children today lack manners, code of ethics, discipline, respect, and moral values. Now placing the blame on these innocent minds are unfair. **Direct blunder should be aimed at the inadequate skills of parenting adults.** I like the catch-phrase on the TV show- **Celebrity Apprentice: "You're fired!!"**

The provision of cell phones, credit cards, driving privileges and free will, exacerbates the dilemma further. The intention of pleasing children has a negative outcome. This procures ample motivation and less incentive, to listen and obey the commands of parents. Why should they bother? You have already release the reigns of designating them with **an adult freelance mentality,** a powerful weapon for children's unprepared immaturity.

At five, I toiled in a laundry six days a week, 365 days per year. I worked diligently, all the way into secondary school (grades nine through twelve). Without a single complaint, or displeasure to my mom. There were nights, when I overheard her crying while ironing. I could not sleep. Helpless is not a word in my vocabulary. In Catholic high school (all girls), I taught my mom the value of purchasing real estate, to escape our poverished lives. Despite the fact I lacked a father figure, **I strategize my financial future.** While the other high school girls had silly mental conceptions of dating, I applied my academic knowledge and business sense, to implement savvy foresights to secure my family's welfare.

These days, children are mean, disrespectful, calculating, and decisively arrogant towards their parents.

Inquiring questions: Are you mentally/physically prepared to be a parent? Am I mature enough to be responsible for another person, for the next eighteen years? Realistically and wholeheartedly ask yourself all these issues.

I am a product of dysfunctional parenting. Embedded are a lifetime of scars, mental torment, suffering, low self-worth, and esteem. Clearly, a lack of purpose prevailed. Adults consumed with their own selfish needs and desires, should think twice before raising a child, who would suffer needless emotional damage, for the rest of their lives.

Every day, young children are being exploited, abused (physically or sexually), neglected, or rejected. All due to the stupidity and callousness of the providers. It is also their careless behavior that puts a child in jeopardy, which can lead to dire consequences. Not to condemn every parent. There are responsible adults who are qualified to provide a loving, nurturing, and caring environment for their children.

Nevertheless, **I place culpability on the women** who unwittingly bring forth children into this world, exposing these unfortunate souls to misery and distress. Based on lack of planning, becoming pregnant at a young age, **or foolish reckless behavior.** I am bewildered to interpret, why women senselessly invite themselves into these predicaments. Discovering later, they have unknowingly committed themselves into a pattern of hardship, sorrow, shattered hopes, and dreams.

Perhaps the answer lies from their own parent's misguided upbringings and ignorances, which led them towards this treacherous path. The cyclical (cycle) disorientation affects one generation onto the next (domino effect). As a result, what is occurring- when one parent sets an example, the child follows in their footsteps. Thereby, it is prudent to stop this vicious cycle, and thwart (block) future disasters from happening.

Make no mistake. **Once becoming a caretaker, there is no turning back.** You are bound to this individual for the rest of your life. **Sorry, no return or exchange policies here.** The role of being a good model- is complex, challenging, demanding, and rewarding. Requiring a lifetime of devotion. It is imperative for all guardians to assume their positions seriously. Uphold the principle and integrity to stimulate young minds, to be good responsible citizens in society. The pivotal chain of sequence, to mold a human's development begins here. Remember this, children are born with pure and wholesome hearts.

It is the sole obligation of the protector to promote and guide their child towards a path of honesty, righteousness, kindness, and harmony in this world. As mature adults, set an example. Inspire them to become productive/pro-active members of society, by **creating a sense of purpose for him or her.**

Aim for good outcomes and results for thyself, and devote yourself to that end, as well as for others. Establishing harmony within ourselves, begins with our own families. Getting along, and working with one another. We can spread that camaraderie towards the community, in achieving a greater atmosphere of well-being all around. Thus, elevating our souls to a higher level.

In retrospect, I never received any form of love from my mother. She was consumed with her miserable outlooks. In sharp contrast, my brother had an outpouring of dedicated love, financial gifts and total devotion, from every fiber of my mother's being. The **dagger to my heart came from her words: "You are an outsider."** At that point, my soul was deeply wounded. I was unhappy, which affected every facet of my well-being.

Unknowingly, I was depressed throughout my daily existence. Whereby, afflicting career and personal relationships. It has takened a lifetime to reverse what I was doing to myself, and commence change. I finally concluded it clouded and impeded my search, for the meaning and actual goals in life.

One of the reasons **I was compelled to write this book-** to forewarn adults, in not committing the horrendous disasters. I wanted to right a wrong. My inner child cried out for all the other neglected, mistreated children. Words cannot express my utter contempt for the irresponsible fathers and mothers. They endanger innocent children to a lengthy risk of hating/ruining themselves, when there were no justifications on their part to begin with. **These unfortunate souls were setup,** the day they arrived. The mental damage includes- blaming ourselves at an early onset, rather than our care providers. Spiraling us towards repeated failures of our unrealistic goals.

Children are born into this world without hatred, bias, guilt, judgments, fair to the core. It is the grown-ups who taint and blind them with the negatives (ambition, dishonesty, selfish behaviors, unhealthy habits, contradictory expectations, etc.). This process derails a child into the direction of self-disappointment.

I am dismayed at some irresponsible parents, who justify their parenting skills by complimenting themselves. Voicing how difficult their tasks were, by demanding children to fulfill the parental roles (asking an older child to babysit, while they attend a social event, forcing young children to work- alleviating the financial burden, etc.).

How do you become a good parent? Teach and raise your child from your heart. Without any ulterior motives from within (cast away selfish desires, goals, and ambitions). Set aside a framework of clear-cut objectives, and positive parenting skills. For the sake of nurturing that child to the fullest extent possible. **Institute good values** (involvement in household chores, money saving tactics), **morals, and responsibility.** Solely for the benefit of his or her best interests.

While the animal kingdom have pack leaders, parents need to be alpha members to guide their offsprings towards the righteous path. Otherwise, they will navigate blindly through life with hits and misses, without fully realizing the outcomes. Let's be honest. **Life is unforgiving** at times, persistently challenging. Imagine how vulnerable children respond, when they are not prepared to face the harsh realities. Fortunately, once children are armed with the proper skills, they will exude with confidence. Confronting life's complexities without any hesitation or trepidation on their part, which makes the journey a lot smoother.

I cannot begin to tell you, how **fear has played a major part in my life.** As a result, I have placed roadblocks in front of me, misdirecting the significance of my being. My mother never taught me the necessary skills, in dealing with the outside world. I limited myself to adventure, experimenting, or exploring new avenues. Entirely from a lack of confidence.

I want to convey to parents- fear and deficient courage is a life-long crippling handicap, where it can devastate one's soul. We need goals to pursue our individual destiny. Without reason, a person is essentially lost, become trapped, and suffocating within their own existence. The same basis applies to suicidal individuals. They have lost their will to live. I do not believe they willingly designate to end their lives. It is an end to a means. As a last resort, to terminate their unsolvable and tragic dilemma (in their eyes).

Children are quite impressionable at a young age. They imitate, absorb, and gravitate towards what the adults are doing. It is pertinent to ensure a solid foundation for the child's developing mind. To effectively deal with life's unpredictable crises. **The objective-** to endeavor cooperative practices- such as fairness, respecting others equally, as an instrument to serve society and humanity.

As humans, **we must implant roots of meaningful values onto ourselves,** if we are to improve mankind's woes and sufferings. It is upon us as individuals to contribute to that cause.
What greater opportunity than to educate and expand that knowledge to a child's pure and innocent mind, a clean slate if you will.

The most dreadful deed a parent perpetrates- by sowing the seed of greed into a child's mindset, perhaps to fulfill their own missed ambitions. This is a deadly arrangement. The end results are maneuverings, manipulations, and dishonesty.

The best legacy parents can bestow onto their children- teaching the ideals of doing good deeds, for generations to follow. We are capable of making the world a better place. Initiation begins with the family structure. The basic building block, of originating a compassionate human being. Sadly, the current family unit has disintegrated over the years, even with today's advance technology. We no longer communicate with one another. We text-message, send e-mails, establishing a cold, emotionless environment.

I treasured the good old days of my generation. Most families convened at the dinner table, discussing their events of the day. Problematic solutions were usually shared with one another. It was therapeutic to resolved the issues together, for the foundation of building trust starts at this crucial level. **Out of trust,** a family can build the groundwork for loyalty and reciprocal respect. An inviting format, to develop skills for a sound marriage. This effect can flow into other aspects of one's life, such as compromise, peaceful negotiations, or forgiveness.

Those early experiences are conducive to facilitating prospective social attributes, in interacting with the world around us. **With regards to major past events, they shape us as individuals, and play an integral part in our future.**

****

A Passage To Intuition

******

Our engaging unceasing competitive world has incrementally decimated our souls. In the daily mask we portray, self-recognition has eroded to a standstill. To survive this hideous onslaught- daily self-awareness of every thought, action, and deed, is the antidote to our answers.

Yes, planet earth is evolving at a rapid pace. Tell thyself: "The source of our being matters, we will all perish one day, left with one infinite possession- our immortal souls."

****The End****

GOOD PARENTING SKILLS

1) Start Good Habits

Train your children near the beginning, to solidify virtuous behaviors. Too frequent, parents hesitate until the teen years to discipline them. By then, it is too late. Teenagers usually do not respond in their rebellious years. They have distinctive priorities, and mindsets.

The basic good habits-

Avoiding drugs, alcohol, gambling, instill benevolent mannerisms, and the clear definition of right and wrong. Missed opportunities can have life altering consequences for the child, and equally devastating for the parents. Appropriate parenting, should commence with proper training in the toddler stage. Children are most receptive to learn at this time.

2) Avoid Favoritism

In the Asian culture, males are preferred over females. Boys are treated favorably, whereas girls are ignored. In my eyes, this is discrimination and unfair. All parents need to treat their children impartially, without any prejudice, or indifference of any kind. Growing up, my mother provided my brother with endless tender loving care, and reverence over me. On the other hand, I was punished for no apparent reason, and scolded most indignantly. Inadvertently, the rationale of: "Never good enough," dominated my mindset.

3) Make Education A Priority

One of the most empowering assets a parent can bestow onto their child- to secure knowledge, and wisdom. I am so blessed, having access to quality education. Knowledge is power, a substantial tool to enhance one's station in life. Education defines who we are, and creates opportunities (financially and emotionally) to benefit and improve our lives.

It is common that most marriage woes are directly related to economic status (arguments connected to lack of money). Earning a college degree allows one to become independent, relying on thyself. Thereby, promoting self-worth, dignity, and self-respect.

4) Quality Time Together

Since we live in a high tech age, life has become increasingly fast-paced and complicated. We have become accustomed to fast foods, drive-bys, e-mails, net-working, tele-conferences, and so forth. This so-called existence has consumed our daily lives, to the point of no return. No wonder, there are high divorce rates, mental breakdowns, mis-communications between one another, and social discord. Despite my sad childhood, I cherished the quality time we shared as a family, albeit a dysfunctional one. Those impressionable moments have no doubt singed (scorch) a permanent imprint on my memory, they are precious to me.

Encourage consistent quality time in meaningful ways-

Such as joining at the dinner table, attending movies, jogging together, doing weekend chores as an entire unit. These activities enforces a sense of belonging. Fostering the next generation to continue this discipline, work ethic, and tradition.

5) Teach Responsibility/Consequences

Adults need to instruct children, to bear responsibility for individual actions. Only then, can they fully accept the consequences of their behaviors. By teaching your child to be a moral being, he or she can impart that knowledge, and set a good example for others to follow. This in turn, leads them on the correct path of righteousness, equality, and kindness for mankind.

6) Implement Values & Traditions

What I find disturbing amongst young teenagers and adults today- they have lost their sense of values and individual selves. Teens are having sex at an earlier age, consuming drugs, and alcohol. As a parent, it is your duty to inform and educate them of the pitfalls, and dangers. I need to emphasize: Parents cannot be good role models, when they themselves are setting a poor example for their children to emulate.

Parents are accountable for the end result of children's wretched conducts. Rules/discussions must be placed, and enforced for realistic positive changes. A family that collaborates in total unison will have a beneficial outcome, and resilience for everyone involved. Traditions (solidarity, trust, loyalty) are based on strong family values, bond, and unity. Inevitably, tested during times of crises. These fortifying links cannot be broken. Once established, becomes permanent and lasting.

7) Safeguard Your Children From Predators

In this day and age, mothers and fathers need to be vigilant. Whether it is at the mall or during a casual stroll. Meanwhile, dangerous predators are canvassing. On the prowl, searching for an opportunistic moment to violate your peaceful existence (abduction). No one is immune to this horrific offense. But take heart, you can supervise control over the situation. Be alert, have a plan at hand. Teach your child to be streetsmart, irregardless of their surroundings.

Care givers- be cautious who the child comes in close contact with, including relatives. Needless to say, do not become complacent. Especially your precious loved ones. Remember, once a tragedy strikes, you cannot undo it.

*** THERE ARE STEPS PARENTS CAN TAKE:**
Initiate a plan of prevention/action, to avert a calamity from occurring:

1) Instruct child not to speak with strangers.
   - If a stranger approaches, walk in the opposite direction.

2) Register your child through "Amber Alert."

3) Teach a young child to memorize emergency phone number and address.

4) When at a mall, do not loose sight of your child.
   - Attach plastic coil wristlets (for toddlers).

SAFEGUARD YOUR CHILDREN FROM PREDATORS

5) Do not leave child unattended.
   - At amusement parks or public restrooms.

6) Avoid entering a stranger's vehicle.
   - Gaze at license plate to obtain description.

7) If being followed, advance to a congested area.
   - Obtain mental image (sex, height, weight).
   - Yell: "Fire!" People will take notice.

8) Be aware of your surroundings.
   - Avoid late hours.
   - When exiting a mall, look behind.
   - Glance inside your car prior to entering, especially at a parking lot or isolated area.

9) Be cautious when entering an elevator.
   - Do not enter alone, if someone looks suspicious.

10) Carry a cell phone for emergencies.

11) God forbid. If child is abducted, instruct him or her to leave DNA evidence behind (removing a strand of hair, scratch surface, bite off a piece of nail, spit saliva, etc.).

12) Do not withdraw from an ATM alone or during late hours.
    - Have a significant other present in the vehicle.

13) Plan a thorough background check on nanny or baby sitter, looks are deceptive.

14) Prepare child with exercises or scenarios for emergencies, abduction, sexual advances, etc.

15) Warn child regarding enticements from strangers.
    - Lure of candy, toys, or money.

16) Do not display name tags on child's back packs or belongings.

17) Predators scan playgrounds for victims, be aware of vehicle being spotted more than once.

18) Teach child exit strategies in different environments, mentally prepare them for chaotic predicaments.

19) Predators are opportunists. Do not leave a child alone in car seat with vehicle on, while performing errands.

8) Teach Contentment

Money and possessions, does not provide happiness. Instead, discontentment promotes the burden of never being satisfied, with what you have or attained. Being poor, provided an immeasurable insight, and humility into my life. The aspect of gratitude was an awakening experience. In essence, a blessing in disguise. The lesson translated- I value love, relationships, trust, and loyalty. These dynamic virtues are essential to sustain my existence.

Having less permits me to treasure the present state of mind. **As a cancer survivor,** health is my utmost priority. I am grateful to be alive! Contentment has freed me. I invest time spent with loved ones, pursue healthy lifestyles, and perform deeds for the betterment of my soul. These self-perpetuating goals has allowed me to be a happy, fruitful person.

9) Initiate Financial Tools

An academic education does not adequately prepare us, for the economic downturns in our unstable business market. **Plan for the financial future-** invest in bonds, IRA's, 401K's, pension funds, money market funds, etc. The wise alternative and key success- is diversifying your entire assets, as a measure to maintain, or increase the profit margins. As the saying goes: "Don't put all the eggs in one basket."

Often times, financial advisors offer pragmatic solutions for the investors. I strongly urge everyone to avoid collateral damage, by listening to their inner voices. Regardless of the opinions suggested, trust thyself with your hard-earned sweat equity. Let me come succinctly to the point:

"Money does not grow on trees."

I grew up with this concept: "A penny saved, is a penny earned." **Allocate the philosophy of financial independence-** in exercising proper techniques of money management (avoiding ponzi schemes), investment strategies (real estate, reliable brand name stocks, etc.). And place this into your mind: "If it's too good to be true, it usually is."

Elaborate to youngsters- the negative impacts of wasteful spending, mismanagement of finance (debts, living beyond one's means, etc.). Set up a minimum bank account for your children. This way, they can appreciate the value of money. Extend their knowledge into other avenues of investing (small business ventures, franchises). **Empower them with tools of monetary self-independence, rather than handouts.**

I get goose bumps reminiscing about my childhood days, selling Kool-Aid out of a make-shift cardboard stand (in front of the laundry). I was charging five cents for each paper cup. **I have a confession.** Instead of disposing those cups, I re-used them for the next customer. Even at age seven, the value of saving transpired through my actions. After a while, they suspected. The cups looked "kinda funny." Thinking back, that was "naughty and not nice." As an adult, I reminded myself not to apply this principle. It was simply wrong.

Finally, **assert control** and supervision over money, not vice versa. The monopoly game of finance is an unnerving volatile, emotional roller coaster ride. Be resourceful, and smart. **Save/ respect your money, and use it carefully.**

10) Do Not Be Spiteful

Teach your children to forgive others. This is one of the vital elements to saving one's soul.

Give clear examples, such as: "Words cannot injure you." By harming others, you are hurting yourself.

I have had many injustices done onto me, during my lifetime. To master the art of compassion, by pardoning others, I have released my burdens of hatred. In retrospect, these experiences were lessons to train my spiritual aptitude. To become more understanding, less judgmental towards others, and be fair. We need to co-exist with one another.

11) Teach Kindness & Compassion

As responsible adults, educate your children to be compassionate to one another. I believe in this wholeheartedly. True inner wisdom is achieved through kind acts, sympathy for others, and treating others as you would like them to treat you. Preaching alone do not suffice. Exemplify behaviors for them to follow. The valuable moral you need to impress- by asserting charitable deeds in life, good fortunes returns to them.

12) Teach Organizational Skills

Life does not have to be complicated. The choice is yours. In today's world, the parent's non-disciplinary behaviors and attributes, have created a chaotic existence for all involved. Invite serenity into your home. Allocate and master your priorities. Tidy up all the insignificant miscellaneous havoc/mess, into a tranquil, soothing restful space (Ah). Plan time appropriately. Consistency is the key, to maintaining an organized environment. A home is supposedly- a sanctuary, refuge, and safe haven from the outside world.

***HELPFUL ORGANIZING TIPS:**

A) Organize sections, one room at a time.

B) Make it enjoyable- a family affair.

C) Teach children to replace items promptly.

D) Assign tasks to each child.

E) Place bins in mud room or play area.

F) Teach children to assist in minor chores.

G) Reward for good efforts: "Good job!"

CHAPTER SEVEN

A MESSAGE FOR TEENAGERS

Forrest Gump: "Life is a box of chocolate, you never know what you're gonna get."

I empathize with every teenager's plight in today's society, and know exactly what you are going through. In kindergarten, a bully (boy) in my class kicked both of my knees, till it bled. The teacher did not come to my aid. Then, for eight years in Catholic elementary school, me and my brother were taunted by adults in the neighborhood, with derogatory gestures, and intonations. There were no school buses in our area. We walked to school every single day. While in Catholic high school, a biology instructor laughed behind my back, and made some unkind remark about me.

Throughout my life, I faced racial discrimination. Not solely from my own culture, but from society as well. The pressure was intense. I had to prove to my mother. By always excelling in school, with first and second honors (in high school), fear of her looking down upon me.

No matter the circumstances, I had an enduring inner strength and held my ground. **Demonstrate your will-power** to overcome the negativity, and **never yield to their level.** Do this by not answering back, walk away from the situation.

Being a young teen is no easy task. I was once a teenager myself. You are vulnerable at that fragile age, always yearning for approval from others. Also, your hormones are out of whack (synchrony), which leaves you with indecision, and poor judgment at times. If you have responsible parents, seek guidance from them. They would do you no wrong.

I was not so fortunate. I did not have a support system. I had to rely on myself. All I can tell you is this. **Remain strong for yourself,** and persevere throughout this tumultuous period. You can weather through those treacherous storms. Build self-confidence in thyself, which enables you to confront difficult matters, later in life. Keep in mind, no one can take your confidence or self-worth from you. Those verbal insults are simply "words," nothing else.

Rationalize their nasty or hateful comments, as an instrument to make you mentally stronger. Apply this thinking to train your mind and thoughts. You need this knowledge to prepare yourself for the real world. As you become stronger, **this inner strength will empower you with such invincibility, no remark can affect you in any way, shape, or form.**

I am very honest about this. Many times, my mother would humiliate my soul to such a degree, my sheer mental will-power, was able to withstand her knife-cutting words. I did not answer back. Eventually, she realized anything she said, had no effect on me. And my mom stopped.

I would like you to **be keenly aware. Embodiment of self-determination** is derived from within, not physical proportions. Exhibit your steadfast stance, and resilience. That alone will defeat them at their own mind game. From this, I hope you will achieve a true sense of self. This becomes the source of guiding light towards your future endeavors, and to set an example for others. Enabling you to grow, and become a mature human being.

Live life to the fullest. **The potentials are endless-** youth, health, and vitality. Be mindful, do not take life for granted. It can easily be taken away from you, anytime. **Always bear this thought- discern from right and wrong.** This is the beacon steering you towards the lengthy journey ahead. When life seems impossible, crumbling all around you, think of it as a means of quantifying your abilities, and values. It is essential to develop your own trust and belief systems. This unseemly world, scrutinizes our core to it's limit.

Reinforce into the mind: "I am in control." Listen to your gut instincts and feelings, for they are never wrong. Do not bow to peer pressure. Focus on your inner soul. Unfaithful and wrong decisions cannot be reversed. Most of all, retain your own individuality with it's flaws and uniqueness. Whatever the outcomes or decisions you decide in life, live with it.

HOW TO DEAL WITH THE OUTSIDE WORLD

1) **Be Resilient-**

Why do others pick on me? There is no single answer. Possibly to deflect their insecurities, low self-worth, and inferiority complexes. Know in your heart- "I am a special, rare person and have something to contribute to the world." Having this knowledge, endeavors you to formulate the resilience to disregard any bias. Replace futile thoughts with creativity (socialize, journaling) and productivity. Become a survivor. Outsmart and outmaneuver their defenses! **Ha! Go tiger!**

Attention: "Teens," Take this for the rest of your life: "Your soul is eternal, not the physical being. Value it with your utmost ability. The dark Lord is plotting, prodding, and provoking to obtain your precious soul." Fulfill your intended destiny with dignity and grace. It is mind over matter!! **Ditto!**

2) **Forgive Yourself-**

It is said, we blamed ourselves for the acts that were perpetrated against us. The valuable lesson to be learned- when you forgive yourself, you are then able to forgive others. I want you to remember this. Do not be hard on yourself. Make concessions, allow some slack. Release the burden within, your soul will thank you. **Thanks!**

3) **Love Your Identity-**

It is vital for youths to have their own identities during these turbulent times. Who am I? How do I develop my own identity? Love and accept yourself with all it's imperfections. Try not to hate thyself. By this, you have set yourself free. You are able to love others, when you appreciate your being first. **I do, I do!**

4) **Keep Your Integrity Intact-**

The mental psyche during the teenage years are especially sensitive. This is a time of resistance, rebellion, attempting to fit in, and belong. Usually, hormones dictates the decisions, rather than common sense. Girls, maintain your virginity for the right guy, or you will regret it. The male testosterones at this stage are in hyper drive. It is difficult for them to foresee the consequences of their actions. **Right on!**

5) **Respect Your Parents-**

I know this is a period of turmoil for adolescents. There are so many times you wish your parents would leave you alone. However, they are providing you with food, shelter, and clothing.

Most importantly, reciprocate your affection with honor. This is invaluable. If you are unable to respect family and yourself, most likely you will lack consideration for others. Invariably, the outside world will also exercise disrespect in return. **Yep!**

6) **Do Not Loose Your Cool-**

When others are unkind to you, my best advice is never reveal your weaknesses. Remain cool, calm, and collective. Avoid the flight or fight response. Infuse behavioral instincts and common sense principles to combat the indecisiveness. Fine-tune your inner wisdom- by not giving into hate, retribution, or spite. If an antagonizing blatant, demeaning statement is directed at you, avoid answering, for you are the stronger opponent. **Yeah!**

7) **Study/Work Hard-**

I cannot emphasize this enough, education is your only way out. You may think school is a tedious daily ritual. In reality, it is a stepping stone in achieving your future goals. That in itself, is freedom in allowing you to aspire to your dreams, and to fulfill those desires. It is imperative for you to do well in your studies. The career field is very competitive in today's world. Education equals independence. In this great country of ours, liberty enables you to become whatever you wish to be. **Yippee!!** Entirely up to you.

8) **Have A Backup Plan-**

I suggest you devise a backup scheme, to implement and prepare for unforeseeable circumstances. Listen to your heart. Ask your inner soul which career will make you happy. Do you have a creative/science/medical/business side? If your parents are domineering and over-bearing. Do not permit them to interfere with your decisions. Furthermore, be wise to mentally secure a foundation for your frame of mind, to establish goals, and ambitions. Once in motion, it solidifies an initiative or plan of action to achieve those objectives. My motto: "Do not run, when you cannot walk." **Go figure!**

9) **Do Not Get Mad Or Even/ Look Good-**

So what do you do, when life gets you down and upset? Do you start binge eating or gorging yourself with food, to release your anger, and frustrations? Listen, that is the incorrect strategy to resolve your problems. You are copping out. The healthy alternative- is to go for a walk or exercise, to release those pent-up stress and emotions. Tell yourself: "I am a good person, I do not need to punish myself." When you appear attractive, you will have the confidence to relate with more important priorities in life. **Look at me now!**

Being in control, means not reacting to volatile situations, and handling it in an adult manner. Thus, displaying an exemplary demeanor for your friends as well. Which in turn, garners you respect and recognition. **Darn tootin right!**

10) Make Good Decisions-

I know some of you are frightened. The pressures of school, and the overwhelming stress that surrounds you. I understand. During these challenging times, internalize safety networks (faith, church groups, support systems), and remain on the right path. You are in total control of your destiny. The choices can forever alter your future, depends on how constructively you choose them. **Oh, well!**

A) Make healthy choices-

Do not excessively drink, smoke, do drugs, and steer clear of steroids. Abandon those violent video games. A real warrior faces the world with courage, integrity, and non-violence. Your reactions, and actions in life has direct consequences. **Gee!**

My advice for teens:

Safeguard and treasure your health, while you are young. Avoid the destructive path of pain and suffering in your later years. Continue devotion, and motivation on your studies. The game of survival- to outwit, and outsmart the temptations awaiting you. **Bring it on!**

B) Avoid getting pregnant-

Resist persuasions and seductions. Stay focused, and concentrate on pursuing your college degree. Become an independent woman, do not depend on a man financially. Here is a wake-up call. Pregnant teens situate along the bracket of poverty and unemployment.

Personally, my strategic implementation took me further than what I had imagined. While in high school, I trained my mom in real estate. By my late twenties, I had a few income-producing, investment properties. I transformed my family's destiny.

Early pregnancy derails any chances of fulfilling your future dreams, and endeavors. Especially during this crucial period, it is most prudent to make wise, intelligent choices. Girls, do you want to live with a lifetime of tormenting thoughts, with: "What if's?"

11) **Beware Of Predators-**

Within the safety net of our inner family circle, there lies a senseless treacherous outside world. Consisting of predators, who's sole purpose is to prey on the innocent and vulnerable, especially naïve adolescents. They may lurk on the internet chatrooms, recreational areas, social events, anywhere. These antisocial demented psychopaths often use creative measures to accomplish their devious plans.

The predator (enemy) is difficult to distinguish, from the general population. In their deceptive guise (appearance) and façade, they portray themselves in a caring manner. Being very approachable, friendly, concerned for your welfare. Add caution- by the enticements of free gifts, secluded meeting places, and warning you to regard the relationship: "A secret." Please, listen to your heart. Your innate instincts are true, and be receptive to those internal alarms.

In this turbulent world, your parents cannot protect you at all times. Adapt, defend, and rely on yourself. This is entirely a learning process. Do not place yourself in precarious scenarios (monitor and do not lose sight of your beverages, they may be tainted).

12) <u>If You Are Bored, Volunteer-</u>

The life of an adolescent has so many ups and downs. They struggle within themselves with self-doubt, esteem issues, where to fit in, and the pressures of whether society accepts them as a whole. When exposed to uncertainty, I suggest focusing your energies towards aspirational outlets, such as volunteering. This is an excellent opportunity to bridge into your future careers, and obtain a sense of the environment, acquire new skills, experiment what is out there to guide you.

I would like to share this- **Happiness is one key in seeking purpose in life.** It is reflected within and can be directed towards others. Sometimes it can be contagious. Furthermore, I believe <u>happiness is a priceless, powerful tool in amassing wealth, success, general well-being, and overall longevity in life.</u>

****<u>LIFE LESSON</u>****

Never, ever give up on yourself!

***<u>TEENS- Figure This</u>:**

"The most impossible things in life are possible."

****

****

<u>A FINAL WORD</u>

******

Preponderance of life is an intricate art and labyrinth. Mastering the techniques requires tremendous insight penetrating skills. It's unpredictability even stymies the most attentive, astute knowledgeable ones. My derived answer: "Opening our twelve channels of the the consciousness realm."

***Preponderance:**

Superiority in quantity, power, importance.

****

****

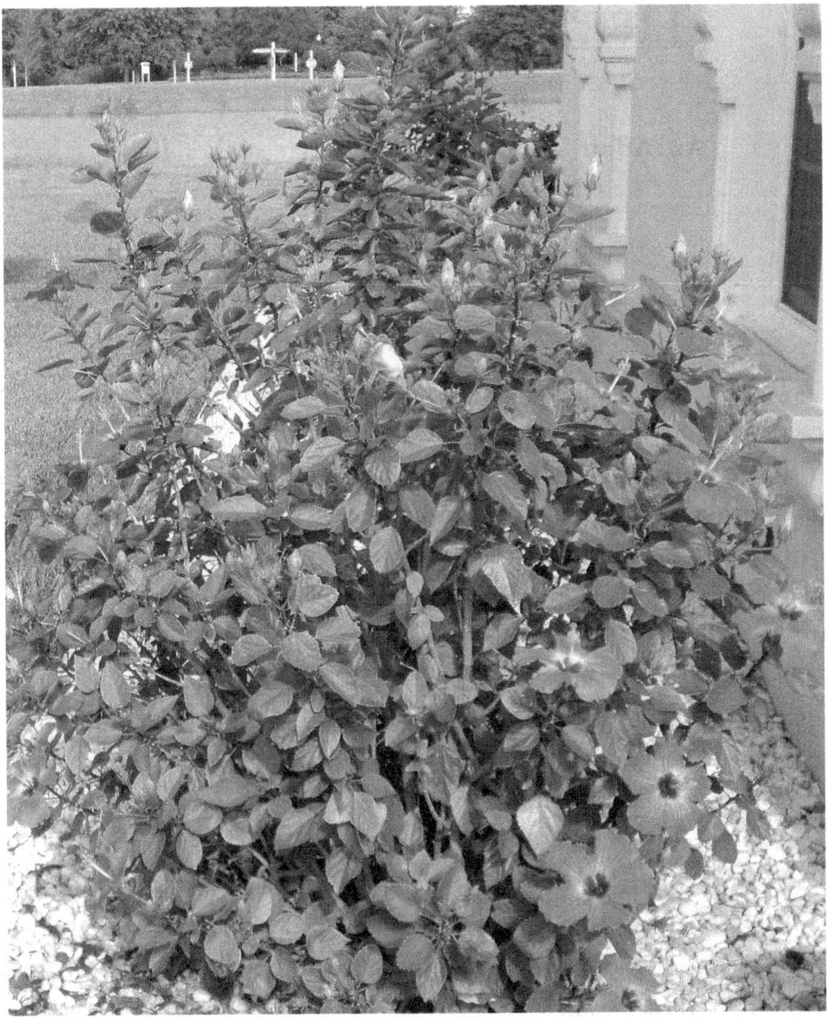

CHAPTER EIGHT

LIFE'S JUST ISN'T FAIR

An Affair To Remember: "What makes life difficult? It's people."

There are so many times in our lives. We questioned why certain experiences do not go our way, or end horribly wrong. **The wheel of destiny plays a major role, signifying those occurrences in conjunction with past-life karmic forces, and present deeds.** The justification (justifying) pattern of life then, unleashes a meticulous interlocking sequence, to deploy cyclical (cycle) jarring incidents into our daily lives.

So what if life is intolerable? Certainly not the end of the world. Confucius once said:

"For every negative outcome, there is an opportunity." I would like you to calm down, and take a couple of deep breaths. Next, re-program your thinking. Sit quietly. Mentally propose a feasible plan to rectify the dilemma. Realize a positive outcome. Your strong determination and perseverance will enable you to endure, and obtain these results.

Believe me, this journey was extremely complex for me. Half a lifetime's labor was necessary to attain fruition. The struggles and deterrents I have encountered were always ever-present. In order to have a confident perspective, I visualized the end results with success. This requires unrelenting patience, and lots of trial and error.

The other unfairness in life: Favoritism, discrimination, and prejudice in the work environment. Nothing is more gut wrenching than inequality. This is a cut-throat world. I have experienced it. No one is immune, nor an inclusive (comprehensive) or specific career target.

The logical plan: Choose a profession you enjoy, navigate a steady course, and do not give up. Even though survival is a basic natural instinct, embedded in our brain functions, do not stray from the path of kindness for others. Select an occupation you will be happy in, that aspires you. Be satisfied, and content in your field. Sensory-overload, misery, and despair are devastating to one's soul. Whereby contaminating your daily existence, and transporting those negative energies into the home environment.

One of the gravest errors: Sacrificing one's integrity and values, for the sake of achieving wealth through any means. The net results are loss of perspective, virtues, namely- self-worth, respect, honesty, and contentment. Preserve the essence (preservation from evil) and wholeness of your soul, to sustain thyself towards the end. **Embody the realization of life- truth and love as supreme over all.**

DISCRIMINATION

A substantial unfairness: Being discriminated for one's race, gender, sexual orientation, handicap, or physical appearance, etc. Life is hard enough as it is. We all desire to survive, and be amicable with everyone in this world. Let alone, being singled out for the very thing that sets each individual apart, our uniqueness and differences.

Despising another human for their very existence, is poisoning the deepest inner sanctum of your being (spirit). **Hatred** is a foul putrid lingering disease. Which can manifest itself, transform, and reconstruct one's purpose into a more pervasive destructive path (violence, malice). God's intentions- he created each and everyone of us as beautiful beings on this earth, to exist with one another.

As an entire race, we need to re-focus. Why not apply this philosophy onto ourselves first? Repair characteristic flaws and resolve issues within, and on the home front. One cannot condemn and criticize others, when he or she has a multitude of problems, imperfections, and even self-hate. The point is: We are all flawed. It is this unique distinction which makes us different.

Re-invent your thinking. Question the inner self: "What is meaningful and valuable for my purpose in life?" You cannot remedy world crises, when the core of your own existence is ailing, and depleted from everyday stress, and anxiety. The primary motive is- heal thyself first. All things will naturally fall into place.

Devise a strategic plan for sense of living early on. Most beneficial of all, **prevail on self-worth, live by it,** and not allowing others to control, or manipulate your direction in life. This is vital in establishing faith within oneself. Effectively, thwarting (block) and preventing undesirable influences, where certain actions or results, can irrevocably alter the path of one's destiny.

When life has dealt you with a negative outcome, do not wither, face the situation with full conviction. Sequester a mood of composure to counter-attack. Dissect the problem, and list steps to resolve the matter. Procure available resources (contacts, organizations, etc.) to expedite the answers. **Trust and rely on your instincts, to guide and lead you towards the end results.**

It is most rewarding, configuring solutions on your own accord. As a matter of fact, rationalize sound decisions, for they are irreversible. Exercise compassion for all injustices. **Christ sacrificed his life on the cross, as an inspiration for others to follow-forgiveness and love.**

HOW TO DEAL WITH RACISM

1) **Think before you react-**
Assess any situation in a calm manner. Avoid physical altercations at all costs. It is not worth it. Do not provide the adversary an excuse to render further blame onto you. If tolerable, merely walk away.

2) **Do not use violence or profanities-**
Always reflect before you speak. I know this can be very difficult, during those intense moments. However, this requires practice and dexterity of mind. Retain this. Verbal insults or damaging statements are irrevocable, and may be used against you in a court of law.

3) **Boycott establishments, that have prejudiced against you-**
Sometimes, people never learned how to treat others with dignity and respect. The logical approach: Is to send a message loud and clear- do not return.

4) **Bill Cosby once said:** "Do you see my skin color? I'm already challenged." I agree wholeheartedly. There are countless times, when life is not fair. We are judged by our individual ethnicity, rather than integrity or character. I have come to a spiritual invoking conclusion. We have pre-determined our journeys, long before we ventured into this world. Think of your life's experiences as a test. Theorize this habitual way of reasoning, as fulfilling and passing those challenges.

5) **Document-**

The pen is mightier than the sword! For each intimidation or abusive verbal attack, record it in a journal. This is therapeutic and practical as well. There is a tendency to be forgetful in an angry state of mind. Use your common sense to record frustrations, alleviate the stress. Release and displace the hurt on paper. Arm yourself with facts, dates, and times. When the opportune period approaches, there is valuable ammunition to defend thyself.

6) **Learn to forgive-**

Regarding forgiveness, this has takened me a lifetime to fine-tune. It is excruciatingly heart wrenching to forgive your enemies. Take baby steps. This is the sound alternative to self-healing. Forgive thyself as well. Pray to God for guidance, in letting go. Gradually over time, it becomes easier to forgive. When finally ready, be sincere from the heart.

7) **Ventilate the hurtful feelings-**

This is very important. Initially, you need to know who to ventilate to. The most beneficial is discussing amongst family members. They can truly empathize your agony and grief. I do not harbor any hatred for any race, even if they had offended me. The fact remains, good and bad exists in every culture.

8) **The pivotal lesson-**

Forgo the stubbornness, even though it is an unpleasant, emotional resounding experience. Relinguish the past and move on with your life. Securing peace of mind/tranquility-necessitates modification of behavioral patterns, attention to details, and altruism. Freedom from hostility and anger, extinguishes the burdens in ones's soul. Imagine your spirit soaring above the earth with unlimited happiness, with an aura of golden light beaming down to greet you. This is the source of power we all hold in our hearts to perform sincere deeds.

9) **Do not blame yourself-**

More often than not, society's unrelenting prejudices starts to invade our minds and spirits. We pondered and begin to blame ourselves for the end result of those obnoxious assaults against us. I want you to alter this behavior, for it is harmful to your psyche.

Instead, embrace your exceptional uniqueness and ethnicity. Respect thyself. Rationalize your special skills, or abilities others lack. I know for a fact. Most minorities are fluent with more than one dialect in their culture. I speak a total of three languages, which I am proud of. Every nationality have their esteem qualities. Begin to appreciate your own self-worth. This is an essential tool in countering the negative remarks being hurled at you. Be proud of your heritage, irregardless of what society perceives of you. Prepare with steadfast confidence, educational/verbal/humanitarian skills, in becoming a worthy, productive, viable member of society. Find the resilience within (it's there).

Envision a frontal invisible protective shield, to tune-off the discouraging feelings, and nasty verbal comments. When you have mastered this technique, remind yourself each time those insults are merely words. Next, pity their actions. They are the weakest links. Fortify your inner strength, with the thoughts of their words as: "Dusts in the wind."

10) Avoid being setup-

Life will inexplicably throw a curve ball, usually when you least expect it. Nevertheless, put forth a transformational plan to modify the mind-set and thinking. Build mental self-confidence to off-set raw emotions or repetitious thoughts. By that, I mean- forgive and pity those individuals for their ignorance, and lack of understanding. They are discontent with their lives.

What does it truly means to be human? The notion which propels us to a higher spiritual level. To fully and honestly forgive others, even when they have hurt us immensely. For this arduous endeavor or task, we can further demonstrate compassion. Then we are worthy of becoming a true human being on this planet. Each time I have endured an unjust episode of discrimination, it motivates me to a greater extent. Reflect in silence, make peace within, and move on.

^^

THEREFORE, I LIKE TO STRESS-

Avoid traps society places upon us:

A) Speed Zones

Be a vigilant and attentive driver to avert these kind of situations. It is my belief they are preventable. The basic principle- pay attention. Unless you are about to give birth in the vehicle, have a valid explanation to get out of this.

B) Contracts

Contracts are a part of our existence. Without one, you can be vulnerable, held accountable for your actions. Prevent a verbal accord, at all costs. They seldom stand in the magistrate of justice. Stipulate demands thoroughly. Document date and time, amount of monetary sum, terms of agreement spelled out, contractual time frame, exclusions, backing-out options, available termination schedules, explicit remedial (supply a remedy) buy-outs, a non-litigation clause for end process, and a respectable attorney. Descriptions should be documented in detail. Include a penalty clause, in preparation if other party breaches the agreement.

Pertaining to an employment contract, review by an attorney is recommended, due to complex jargons, and intricate wording contents.

When mailing an enclosed contract, implement certified mail with receipt. Cover your bases, with statements. Such as total, no hidden costs, and specify additional agreement terms in the addendum.

C) Avoid Financial Scams

Do not trust anyone, with your hard-earned money. This includes relatives and friends as well. Unfortunately, it is the reality of life. A common saying: "There is a sucker born every minute." By reason of falling prey to greed. Ask yourself: "If it's too good to be true, it usually is." The basic core- if people did not possess excessive desires, they would not become vulnerable to these regrettable schemes.

Do not be lazy. Contact the BBB (Better Business Bureau) to investigate the firm's reputation and standing. Once the money leaves your hand, it is exceedingly difficult to retrieve it back. Play it safe, charge purchases with a credit card, for future recourse. Finally, check your monthly statements for any discrepancies.

C) AVOID FINANCIAL SCAMS

*****GLANCE FOR THE FOLLOWING RED FLAGS:**

1) Do not hesitate.
2) I need your answer.
3) Must respond now/promptly.
4) Send a check in the amount of.
5) Wire X amount of money overseas.
6) Your investment will increase.
7) You are a select few to receive this.
8) The opportunity ends by a certain date.
9) You will not be disappointed.
10) There is a money back guarantee.
11) This is the chance of a lifetime.
12) Do not make the mistake of your life.
13) You will receive a monthly statement.

14) Do not tell anyone else about this great offer.
15) Need a down payment/deposit for the prize or gift.

D) Purchasing Real Estate

Buying a home is one of the greatest investment purchases in life. Hence, this should not be taken lightly. My motto is: "Location, location, location." And a desirable spacious kitchen floor plan, it is the focal point in a household. Avoid close proximity to highways, cemeterys, land fills, utility poles or stations, for these all have negative feng shui.

Realtors:

From personal experience, I have come acrossed some unscrupulous agents. Who were solely interested in their individual pockets, benefits, with total disregard for the homebuyer. I am certain there are realtors, who have the utmost integrity and diligence. Good luck, if you can locate a decent one. Property values in the erratic real estate market can vary and fluctuate, according to each area (prime locations).

Commissions:

For my preference, I prefer to look at a prospective property myself. There are more negotiating powers with regards to commissions. With an agent, she or he collects all the profits. Utilize the internet or newspapers for your research, including drive-bys (if time is permitted). If you are dependent on an agent, for a career transfer, interview at least three realtors, to ascertain some input. The greedy ones, usually demand a higher percentage. Stay away from one year lengthy contracts, the maximum should be six months. This is for your own protection (as backup for future mishaps). You can ask for an extension later on. There are always surprises! Associate realtors from local churches or synagogues. They usually have a reputation to uphold, and reluctant to tarnish their credibility.

Deciding Factors:

There are three basic driving forces:

1. A suburban community with a spacious property for solitude.
2. City living for convenient commuting.
3. School districts for children.

Either way, **visit the existing community.** Knock on doors, interview the current homeowners, to obtain an overview of the positive and negative aspects. Based on my own trials, you will be surprised how honest these people can be.

The resourceful information can inform of any pitfalls, litigation matters with the Homeowner's Association (if any), the building of a new highway expansion, builder's conundrums, home disputes, and safety issues. Nowadays, depending on certain areas, you need to visit the property during late hours, to fully discern the realistic activities of the neighborhood.

Renovations:

Additionally, if there are no intentions to inhabit a property for the next ten years, please do not initiate any renovation projects. Due to unpredictable natures and circumstances, it's difficult to determine the actual amount you can recoup from the investment. **The practical and economic approach,** is through cosmetic interventions (painting, new tiles, changing faucets, lighting fixtures, or updating the window blinds, etc.).

Important Choices:

I once made the critical error of building a new custom home, in the rural area. When it was time to sell, only a few select buyers were available. The usual ploy is bargaining for a lower figure. It did not matter that my home had many top of the line, beneficial amenities. These persnickety (picky) purchasers simply overlooked everything, and attempted to low-ball the selling price. Therefore, be very cautious where you plan to construct your new residence. At times, your career dictates the length of stay, not vice versa.

Contracts

For custom construction, it is critical to locate a competent and reliable builder. Forsake the Yellow Pages. Instead, view comparable local home builders in the area. Obtain references from realtors and homeowners in your particular community. They tend to be the most accurate resources. The vital component, is the contract between homebuyer and builder. Never, ever believe the completion date he provides you. Each home that I have purchased, had consistent delays and circumstances, that affected the actual outcome of the date.

Contracts:

In most instances, these binding contracts tend to be lengthy, wordy, overbearing, and in favor of the builder's self-interests, and bottom-line profits. Go figure, they were probably drafted by attorneys. No warm and fuzzy feelings here. Normally, there is insufficient protection for the prospective homebuyers. However, to anchor a safety net in your favor, demand and **stipulate a penalty clause** into the contract. Documenting X amount of days, to ensure that the home is completed in a timely manner.

Likewise, incorporate the realtor's commission fee (if there is one) and the builder's into the contract. Avoiding future disagreements between the two parties. **Include in detail,** any extraneous work into the addendum, the specific monetary amount agreed upon (an extra deck, pool, include spare paints, tiles as well).

First and foremost, before you sign any document, **validate the reputation of the builder** through the Home Builder's Association. Word of mouth is inadequate. By all means, inquire about his license and bonded certificate, and that he has not sustained any liens against him. In the event, there is a ramification on your hands in the distant. Have the contract reviewed by an attorney, for oversight.

It is **contingent** to combine a clause into the contract, to acquire a home inspection of your own selection, prior to closing. If he adamantly opposes, it's a major red flag. Seek another builder. A competent builder would easily comply. <u>Specify in writing-</u> intermittent walk-throughs and inspections with the builder or construction supervisor during the structuring phase, to avoid any miscommunications or delays.

<u>Home Inspections:</u>

Do not utilize home inspectors recommended by the realtor or builder, in avoiding any conflicts of interests. **Hire your own.** Check if he is accredited with his affiliation. Interview at least two, to gain a perspective into their activities. A reliable inspector provides three examinations: Initial, mid-way, and final. Believe me, this is well worth the expense.

The Final Walk-Through:

This is the most decisive and **final phase** of the home purchase. Why? You are holding the builder accountable for any missteps or loopholes discovered during the building process (plumbing issues, structural defects, heating, A/C- air conditioning, or cosmetic problems, etc.). Do not rely completely on the inspection report. Since this is a major purchase in a lifetime, I suggest thoroughly inspecting the exterior and interior with the builder or supervisor yourself. Accompany a significant other or witness for moral support.

Secure a notepad, write down every **detail of the home** that is unsatisfactory. List in an organized format, starting with the exterior, then the interior. Observe for visual cracks on the outside structure, especially the driveway. Ascertain if the grading is sloping downwards. During a rainy downpour, this prevents water from receding into the foundation. Gutters and downspouts are also vital in draining water away from one's property. Averting mold issues in the later years.

Be aware of any **encroachment debates** concerning the lot or boundary lines in the property. This information is essential in preventing landscaping, renovation projects, and neighbor disputes in the foreseeable future.

Regarding the **final inspection of the interior,** pay close attention to the plumbing, heating, air conditioning, and electrical. An oversight can contribute, exorbitant costly repairs down the road. Turn on every faucet, inspect the water flow, especially the shower areas. Flush each toilet as you go. Test all the electrical outlets. Carry your floor plans, to evaluate exact areas, for the cable and telephone locations. Examine, open the furnace/water heater, and inspect the interior flames.

Bring along **painter's tape.** Mark areas where paint touch-ups or cosmetic flaws, needs to be addressed. It is a good idea to glance at the floor designs. This provides the visual effects, to determine if everything was promised in the construction. For instance, my builder neglected to include the Corian counter board and touch-up kit in the final walk-through.

Operate the dishwasher during the inspection, check for any leaks. Open and close every window, or garage door. Present the inspection report, to pinpoint defects noted by the home inspector. **Document explicitly,** a time frame in completing the "punch list." Obtain a copy of that list. Always remember, execute all pertinent notes in writing. That's the golden rule. Lastly, enjoy your new home.

Get It In Writing:

One of the disastrous mistakes people repeatedly make in life- a verbal agreement amongst friends, associates, and families. It usually returns to bite them (ouch!). When money squabbles arises, the long enduring relationships can suddenly evaporate. You are left with the harsh reality for being stupid and naïve.

POEM

Life Is A Game

Life is a game of chess
It all amounts to just a test

There's a maze of twists and turns
Relative to how life churns

This is no simple matter
For there are consequences after

Make careful crucial choices
They will affect your inner voices

Life is not a joke
Take the valuable lessons and let it soak

Learn to forgive and forget
This will ease the burdens & put your mind at rest

When things are chaotic, find solitude
Because you will have a better attitude

Once the journey is over
Those deeds determines our fate forever

Please, do not make irrational mistakes
Be vigilant, for Christ's sake

CHAPTER NINE

YOUR SIXTH SENSE

The Sound of Music:
"Nothing comes from nothing."

The sixth sense is defined as a power of perception, seemingly independent of the five senses (sight, smell, hear, taste, and touch), that is intuition. To a degree, we all possess it, some more than others. In my case, I had a heightened sixth sense since childhood. The ability to bring all these senses to an accelerated level is possible. As an example, I am able to use my sight beyond just seeing, per se. I can surpass to the next elevation.

By implementing inner wisdom eye, in visualizing clarity into my life's journey, and as a source guide. For smell, **I am able to detect** minute traces of gas odors, thus preventing a hazardous explosion in my mother's basement. In hearing, I can discern sounds while I am sleeping (I'm asleep, yet I hear my husband when he leaves and shuts the door). In taste, I am intuitive in avoiding certain foods that are not agreeable (in mental/vision form). When I touch someone or something, I assert a good sense of accurate judgment skills pertaining to the person, or inanimate object.

How is this all possible? The answer may surprise you, yet quite simple. The dominating precept (rule) required, is garnering a truly benevolent heart. Being nice does not qualify. Nope. **What does it mean to have a pure heart?** This is most arduous to achieve. The heart is void of hatred, spitefulness, jealousy, meanness, lust, and addiction within thyself. These are all deterrent traits, which obscures the meaningful luminescence we wish to see. When a person is consumed with loathing, their vision is clouded with this destructive force. Disabling the individual from seeking true wisdom or answers in life.

I say this, with straight forward sincerity from my heart. With truthful honesty within, to deepen your understanding, how this can be achieved. This has been a life-long journey of mine. Forgiving others, whether racist, malicious, or out of spite. **True knowledge is derived** from the ability to heartedly excuse another human being. Pity them, for they lacked fortitude of spiritual wisdom.

Let me elaborate further. Do you have the mindset and heart of a young child (an eight year old), with the maturity of an elderly wise sage, in an adult body? Is this even plausible? Not impossible, I am living proof. In the majority of cases, children reach adulthood with hearts and souls tainted. Thereby, highly improbable they will enter the kingdom of heaven in their lifetime.

Guess what? Even with the mentality of a child, you are only halfway in goal, towards navigating through the difficult pathways of life, and challenges God has set forth, for each of us. The feng shui experts have quoted life as 80 to 90% adversary (does not go our way). The remaining 10 to 20% offers happiness (our wishes come true). There are immeasurable roadblocks that interferes with everyone's journey. **Mental concentration skills and determination, are the necessary sources of discipline required.**

Why is it critical to have an innocence and pureness of heart? This has taken me a lengthy time to decipher. The essence of purity allows accessed flow of information. There are literally thousands of wisdom concepts passing through speed of light, undetectable or noticeable to the human eye. In order to retrieve the information, it requires a milli-second in time to grasp that source. What is milli-second? It is one-thousandth of a second.

There is a **direct relationship between sixth sense and wisdom.** With each extensive test we pass in life, the more spiritually advanced one becomes. Along with this knowledge, I can utilize all my five senses simultaneously, to isolate and dissect the problematic puzzles of existence, or dilemmas I am faced with. This adeptness has allowed wisdom, to receive me at my beckoned calls. Unnecessary to search for it. Which explains why I seldom rely on self-help books, or seek advice from others. The real answers are accessible to me.

Throughout my life, my hard-learned lessons have solidified these beliefs. The powers of wisdom has enabled me to defy the surmountable odds, stacked against me. The greater number of life's obstacle course, requires accurate judgment dexterities. Frequently, there are no second chances. **Armed with the ammunition of sixth sense and wisdom,** one can become a formidable force to be reckoned with. Never underestimate the dark lethal demonic powers, in response to attack in all directions.

I could have been easily consumed with animosity, from being continuously exposed by it's prevailing negativity. **My father hated and resented me. My mother never loved me.** Society did not showed much compassion either. Without a support system, I carried on, to successfully come out this unscathed. With sheer tenacity, I did not yield. All the while maintaining a pure heart, being cautious my soul was not tainted. I have never considered myself a bright person. However, awaken wisdom exceeds intellectual capabilities.

In hindsight, I strategically planned a sheltered monastic life long ago. Living in religious seclusion, avoiding unnecessary traps. Make no mistake, I endured indefinite hardships along the way. I suffered in silence, the sneers, shame, and ridicule from family. In Chinese culture, unproductiveness is viewed as: "A worthless human being." I ceaselessly cried in tormenting pain many times over, in deafening solitude. Knowing my journey would not be effortless, yet I persevered.

Life is often about sacrifices, they may entailed the exact opposite of what society expects of you. Not trusting others became an invaluable asset to me, I trusted myself. By forsaking my career, money, or other earthly treasures, God have granted spiritual credits for my life-long endurance. Humans are repeatedly misled, making disastrous decisions.

Wisdom defies scientific or medical explanations, even logic and reasoning; beyond comprehension. It also mystifies the imagination, because you are elevated to a dominant status. Having the ability to interpret another being's insights, thoughts, and their very soul. I have the capacity to view through a person's soul, even from meeting the individual for the very first time. What God has bestowed onto me, is his great love for Mae Louis. My soul is eternally grateful. The clarity is apparent. I serve God and no one else.

One cannot even begin to realize the real importance of life, or embrace true consciousness, without first opening the door of wisdom. Excavating it's paramount essence of information. Once revealed, you will see the world in a totally different concept, thyself, and one's existence. Mankind or sentient beings (humans), are living within their **matrix realm of life,** oblivious to real implications of individual deeds, actions, or motives. Such blind-sightedness inhibits the mind-spirit duality, from even reaching the initial phase of one's awakening. The lure of temporary short-term materialistic endeavors, further hinders the progress.

We all entered into this world with insignificance, and will leave with nonexistence (not existing). The majority realizes the difference between right and wrong. Yet, unable to resist temptations of wants and needs, all due to lack of intuitive wisdom. Spiritual insight resonates one to focus on realistic expectations, from false deceptions. That accounts for one quarter of the journey. **The rest reverberates on** compassion, good deeds, forgiveness, continual spiritual self-improvement, being true to thyself, and living a non-sinful lifestyle.

The compelling path towards deepening the sixth senses, requires a genuine contemplative conscious level, on a daily basis to have self-awareness, realization of our individual actions, and deeds. This is one method of discovering your true soul. Correcting the flaws and mistakes inherent in all of us, is an extensive consuming ordeal. One needs to question their own motives to determine whether it was based upon integrity, principle, or false perception. Do the actions justify the means? This is the question you need to ask yourself. Was it righteous and fair? Weigh the thoughts with your conscience, for it will guide you towards the right direction.

Subject yourself to a role-reversal. How would you feel if this deed was perpetrated onto you? Always be considerate of the other person. If there were deplorable acts committed recently, correct them promptly. Do not hesitate or delay for any length of time. Another fortunate opportunity may not exist. Seize the moment. These mental exercises are resourceful tools to train ourselves to become self-reliant towards the complex outside world, and to rectify the continual on-going problems we face every day.

The next strategy- avoid repetitive or sinful errors. We all have our foibles (weaknesses), no one on this planet is perfect. A foreboding warning: Rehearsing and thinking of past hurtful experiences, as if duplicating the mental scars, will deter one's spirituality from entering the celestial spheres of light. Rendering a complete waste of precious time. Valuable energy should be directed to other mindful, insightful purposes.

Another **major blundering obstacle, blurring one's path-** monetary interests. This delicate matter, always detrimentally strike close to our ignorant hearts. It affects our very existence. The source of evil and misery, throughout history to the present, has always been connected with money. The resolution: Not allowing the commodity control you. We are masters of our destinies. That choice defines the actual outcome.

With expeditious sixth sense application in daily practice, I can recognize my weaknesses. Then formulate a strategy, maximize it to my utmost advantage. **Case in point:** I have a limited social interaction with society. Still, I am cognizant of the exterior world, within it's intricate and minuscule (small/minute) patterns. I have been receptive to warnings, at no particular juncture in time.

Until now, no one has ever suspected, I have visualized eventual outcomes in advance. For example, I instinctively sold my home, prior to the real estate fiasco. There were many episodes, where I had no clue an incident had actually occurred. Yet, I was able to realize the very instant it happened. There is no scientific explanation for this phenomenon. Except to believe a divine presence (God or True Source) is orchestrating this.

EARTHLY WORLD VS. SPIRITUAL WORLD

The apex of securing advanced spiritual knowledge- allows one to realize there is a definitive cause and effect between the earthly, and spiritual world. This awareness is evolved from intensive thought provoking/soul searching, analytical, and philosophical skills mastered, and manifested through one's lifetime. Notwithstanding, unbeknownst to the average person, wisdom is all-knowing.

Every living person have prior journeys to the current one. Hence, the knowledge which dwells within us, once unlocked, contains a vast extraordinary source of unlimited supreme possibilities, beyond our own expectations. **What I am about to reveal is a real awakening to your senses, and self-actualization (realize in action) between reality and consciousness attunement (to tune).**

EARTHLY WORLD

We all have embarked upon the world through our mother's wombs. No one can dispute this. With it, a family unit is formed. In our environment, one is exposed to all sorts of spirals and turns (they are the traps of life). There are seductions of greed, lust, hate, jealousy, awaiting in our paths. **What distinguishes our fate is the choice between lightness (good) and darkness (evil).** Incumbent upon one's upbringing, association or environmental exposure, an individual has the free affirmative to facilitate his or her judgment protocols. No one dictates our decisions or forces it upon us. As a result, cause and effect are based intrinsically (inherent) on our actions. With this in mind, the human brain is equipped with absorbing expandable knowledge: By way of books, spirituality, and valuable informed experiences. Eventually reaching the highest realm, which is true inner wisdom.

Wisdom is directly related within everyone's soul, whose expansive awareness spans many lifetimes and journeys. This explains when someone is declared a child prodigy, or gifted at an early age. Evidently, throughout each experience, we are deluded by jagged edges and rough currents, that either strengthens or weakens our resolve. There are no coincidences, whatever trivial the situation may be. Perplexing (confusing) on the surface, with discernable truths of wisdom beneath. **Life's complicated juxtaposing (side by side) maze, consists of a purpose within a purpose.**

EARTHLY WORLD

Now, allow me to truly open your eyes. Your so-called earthly families, are not really families. They are merely distractions, directed at confusing our motives in life. As intentional ploys to propel us off-course. In any given family structure, there are **four emotional elements involved: Love, hate, jealousy, and resentment.** These connected factors, determines or shape our characteristics.

Ultimately, playing a powerful delineated role in our decision-making processes. From there, are judgmental skills that requires a precise, careful implemented course of action, in executing the harmonious righteous path towards our life cycle. When completed, is always reflected back onto ourselves. Most do not comprehend this. It's simplistic form of understanding is apparent to everyone, they prefer to turn their backs on ignorance.

The earthly world consists of numerous inviting pitfalls (greed, vanity, materialistic possessions, lust, etc.). Darkness is constantly inundating, and reminding us of the temporary pleasures at hand. Enticing some to the point of no return. TV ads, magazines, tempt our minds with the plethora of fantasy, unrealistic hopes, dreams, and desires to devour the very existence of our souls.

SPIRITUAL WORLD

I come to my favorite topic, the spiritual world. The **sphere is of celestial (divine) nature, which defies time and space.** Those admitted into this realm, have mastered their far-reaching/extended bountiful knowledges and experiences. Attainment of advance spiritual endowments, allows passage into this prodigious kingdom sanctuary of perpetual/exuberant bliss, wonderment, free of disease, humanistic frailties (failings) or weaknesses, at peace eternally. Every soul that inhabits this plane co-exist in heavenly unison, and harmony.

There is no bodily figure or necessity to compete. Sex is unimportant, and non-existent. The worldly possessions are gone. This is where one has finally achieved true spiritual fulfillment to the absolute degree. Nothingness is present, utter luminous clarity of mind/wisdom/soul is intertwined in synchronous totality. Absence of any downfall measurements, unlike the qualities of a living being.

The essence of pure hearted souls persists on this dimension, reserved for such divine beings- Angels, Saints, and Godly figures. You can join this entity as well, free will. The choice is entirely yours. I have mentioned this before: "It is far easier to become a bad person, than a good person." The uphill journey is well worth the sacrifices and grueling tests, to gain permission into the kingdom of perpetual serene happiness.

Total awareness of stupendous aptitude, secures a seat in the holy phoenix of spiritual gifts. The all-knowing attributes is attuned with the ability to solicit pertinent information at random. Visualizing the entire soul's journey- from beginning to end. Remember, I stated: "A family is not truly your family." The all-seeing soul can meticulously and incrementally determine in slow motion, re-wind what had culminated up to this point in time. The rationale for every event that had occurred.

The beings we have encountered in human form, were arranged by a specific consecutive order, and positioned in the life cycle continuum. Each juncture of the daily living, sequence of events, trials and tribulations, had an accurate role in affecting our motives, actions, and behaviors as a being.

Using sixth sense logic, one can effectively monitor and evaluate the current progress in present life, by intermittently questioning deed, self-worth, and integrity. This ability formulates the groundwork for improving spiritual growth towards the higher wisdom/ knowledge path. These mental exercises are instrumental tools- to culminate inner insight perspective, and connecting with conscience. Thereby tapping into compassion, in order to be awakened. **And that reason is the prime source of spiritual truth.** The stages of spiritual development evolves through a myriad of lifetimes. The overwhelming deciding factor involving ones's journey- having total faith and a confident belief in God, True Source, Buddha, Allah, etc.

Allegiance to God encompasses no shred of doubt, skepticism, or pondering. A simple analogy: **"For you to believe in something, you must trust, that is the logical basis of faith."**
Religious belief has a mysterious aura, aimed to lead and guide us towards the right direction. Those without faith are confounded with indecisiveness, enduring repetitious miscalculations in the life cycle. We all question our loyalties to our faith, to justify if it is genuine or not. Saint Faustina even had doubts, and needed reassurance from God. They were answered by visits from God and the Angelic Saints above.

When Quan Yin (Goddess of Compassion) appeared before me, I knew instantaneously it was no illusion. I was not losing my mind. I was completely awake and alert (free of any drugs), when I received the divine apparition. One night (on another occasion), I was preparing to go to bed. As I closed my eyes, I saw a vision of a golden Angel for one minute. I blinked the second time, the Angel disappeared.

These holy affirmations are intended as confirmations, for our honest devotions. It is a sacred privilege to be worthy of being greeted, by the appearances of these Saintly figures. **This reinforces my belief system, as a profound meaningful segway, in the directional path of the white light.**

Solid bond and trust in God, is a powerful ethereal (heavenly) connection to our almighty Lord. He conveys love and compassion, for those who desire to achieve salvation. Going to weekly mass and being mean to others, negates the purpose. This requires more than your entire being to completely embrace and practice God's teachings, through one's deeds. From personal experience, I can share this. Your doubts, questions, fears will vanish, circumstantial evidence prevails, to prove otherwise. A higher authority persists to alleviate the vulnerabilities, that plagues and puts forth false expectations in our hearts.

One sunny day. On June 2010, we were in our vehicle on our way home, in a two lane road. Suddenly, a car in the opposite direction, was navigating straight towards us, for a head-on collision. I immediately shouted: "God!". Instantly, the driver turned his steering wheel to correct himself, and resumed on his lane. As if a force had overtaken and awakened him, at that exact moment in time. We both witnessed the unexplainable incident. I have no uncertainty in my mind, **this was a divine intervention.** Simply not my time to go. An integral intentional purpose was reserved for me (to complete this book). This exclusive spiritual revelation-reckoning, is a valid tangible basis for belief. God protects those who have faith in him.

Devout Buddhist monks have devoted their entire existence towards faith. There is a phenomenal attribute, they are hesitant to reveal. I am aware (with exceptional spiritual achievement), **some (their soul) can travel to other dimensions.** Via deep meditation or a complex contemplative state of mind. How is this possible? Absolutely feasible. I have been there myself, without any compromise. Please, this is not a joke, definitely true.

We have the ability to visit the dimensions between heaven, and hell. For those lacking in faith, they will never conceive, or glimpse such a nuance. **The requisites-** deep faith and an unequivocal compassionate sense of reasoning, multi-intuitive qualities, wisdom eye stature, to accomplish this state.

When I was twelve years old, I had a vision of hell, it exists. The "Tibetan Book of The Dead" states: "When a being leaves his bodily presence, he is tested in the afterlife for seven days." I can attest to what I have already seen. And acknowledge **our reasons** here on this earth, **comprises of intention and significance, geared towards seeking true salvation, and final return to the state of origin.**

1) ULTIMATE TRUE WISDOM

Again, there are stages one needs to follow, in order to achieve the highest level- ultimate true wisdom. **First awakening** is the crucial step. **Next,** the mind, spirit, wisdom, soul connection, has to be in unison to be receptive and accepted into the spiritual dominion of the Universe. Levitating towards greater holy advancement.

To possess ultimate true wisdom is an awesome power indeed. The characteristics or traits are all-knowing truth (since I have already attained true thyself), implementing invisible shield to protect myself, utilizing space-travel via the mind, and advanced sixth sense capability. By wisdom truth, I mean being a human lie detector. There is no second guessing, infinitely precise and exact. By merely peering into one's eyes, I can decipher whether the person is lying or saying the truth. **According to space-travel,** I can go anywhere I desire without boarding a plane for my destination. I have traversed to the pyramids of Egypt. The Eiffel Tower in France (I literally see the massive iron beam structure), the giant Buddha in China. **All via my soul,** minus the expense and hassles of transportation.

Regarding **superfluous sixth sense capability,** one is able to read a person's mind and soul at the identical time. I am acutely aware of past, present, and future. During my past, I was English and Italian in previous lifetimes. This explains my love for English history, fashion, and architecture. I immensely enjoy eating pizza and pasta **(mama mia!).**

Somehow, I am able to predict present or future events, lacking any control of my own. This simply happens, I cannot explain it. The predictions have become so accurate, I no longer dismiss my abilities. My gifts are primarily utilized to facilitate others.

Paradoxically, by accidental occurrence, I happened to receive messages from other souls in the dream state. **Case in point:** My husband was interviewed by a female physician. I asked my wisdom regarding the outcome. Her soul divulged to me: "I've already made up my mind, he won't be hired." Needless to say, he never obtained the position.

I also have a telepathic connection with animals. Here is the evidence. My spouse divulged to one person at a conference, that I can communicate with animals. He asked: "What proof do you have?" My husband did not have one, and said: "She does." A few months later, we attended a meeting together. This same individual was present at the seminar as well. Usually, there are no animals at these sessions. That day, there was a guide dog with it's owner. During a break, unbeknownst to me, I met this dog and saw her eyes. Normally, I am a shy person. I told the dog owner: "Your dog is thirsty." I disclosed to my husband, regarding the strange encounter.

Later, we had another break. Out of curiosity, my husband boldly approached the dog owner (only one dog during the entire lecture). He inquired if her dog was thirsty. She replied: "Yes, she was very thirsty, normally she isn't this parched, thank you."

My husband also revealed to the same man, who doubted my mystical telepathic skills. And relayed this experience to him. He laughed, and didn't dare to question my ability again. This is a clear instance, how almighty God intervenes mysteriously, and reinforces my beliefs beyond skepticism.

<u>I recently took up Tai Chi lessons.</u> With insufficient time, I resort to this method. I perform a quick automatic DVD image rewind, on my mind, from half an hour, to a few minutes. How is this even possible? I have previously practiced this mental exercise, many times. It works. I lie on a flat (supine) position, void of any

extra-sensory interruptions. While I am concentrating, I actually feel the **chi (life force energy)** circulating throughout my entire body. The pulsating nerves flickering about. The vital step is- having an advanced photographic memory dexterity to achieve this. Without the photographic proficiency, it is render useless and ineffective.

To master the inner circle secrets of Tai Chi, is exceedingly mind astounding. I found a gateway. I have entered the dominion of it's secluded, spiritual hidden world. The flux and fluidity of energy sequence, is determined by applying forms with light feathery strokes, with ease. At the same moment, **continually strike with precision-force dexterity of scissor-like hands, by slicing a piece of paper.**

It is no coincidence, abundant wisdom has permitted me to uncover the complex interlocking maneuvers, other pinnacled Tai Chi Masters have achieved from previous centuries. **The ebb (decline) and flow of each synergy (sense) movement, is unanimously in tune with continuous total mind/body relaxation.** Yet, I am a novice. As strange as this may sound, innovative moves never introduced to me before, I can manifest new inventive depth-provoking strokes, from out of nowhere.

Not withstanding, **I implemented a process of self "thermo-regulation."** Whereby, during episodes of sweating in Tai Chi, I thermostatically diffuse and lower my body temperature at a comfortable level. Within a matter of minutes, this is accomplished.

I know you may be eager to ask. **What does God look like? Here is the answer.** He consists of an enormous bright golden light, without body or form. There is no physical presence. Apparently, God can astutely culminate into any form he desires. When I hug

God, he provides the most exulted context of love a person can even possibly receive or feel. I sense the warmth of his embrace (from my soul). And no, God does not converse with me. I am grateful, his mere presence alone is sufficient enough.

This arrived from nowhere. Again, it just happened. My will was so great and immense. Without difficulty, **I travel to God's heavenly dimensional echelon to greet him (by soul).** It is an astonishing exuberant comfort, beyond explanation. To be immersed with the intense light, brought about unimaginable peace and calmness into my soul. When I am deeply troubled, I gravitate freely to receive his amazing indelible reassurances.

Let me ask you. **Can you control your dreams?** If the answer is no, then you have not attained advanced spiritual growth. If yes, know that in these image sequences, we are being tested on a subconscious level. Dreams are not alone by reason, revelations about our thinking or thought patterns. Merely part of it. If you can interpret, dreams reveal future occurrences. In one of my self-controlled dreams, I fly mid-air out of harm's way, from my adversaries **(I'm able to receive future insightful receptions, in a nano-second in time).**

Events take place in everyone's cycle. Simply examine certain past experiences, that have been repeated. **The innermost memory vortex (whirlpool), contain life lessons** (deja-vu incidents). Recollections, to be grasped, extrapolated and siphoned, as means to guide ourselves towards the next step.

<u>FURTHER ELABORATIONS OF INVISIBLE SHIELD</u>

This is a reiteration. **An additional exploration into invisible shield, which I had invented solely by myself.** It was not by coincidence, that I derived this. There is a meaningful purpose. If you recalled in a previous chapter, I had a vision of my grandmother in hell. I finally released her soul, she patiently waited for fifty-one years.

Afterwards, I realized the dark forces would be antagonistic towards the intervention. I was solemnly concerned, and inquired my wisdom. A short time later, I instinctively projected an invisible shield, encapsulating my entire physical body (for life), as a protective armor from evil presence. Coincidently, **not anyone can perform invisible shield upon themselves or others.** It's only validated through God, and whether a person is deemed worthy to receive. The intention must be conceived from pure spirit status, to be effectively manifested to True Source, and the honorable state of mind to assist others. Self-serving ambitions, or tactics of sustaining fame and notoriety, garners empty results.

Obviously, at first I was perplexed whether the protective shield would function or not. Since my faith in God was steadfast strong and resilient, fruition became a reality. On January 2009, we had a winter freeze for eleven days straight (in Florida). **I positioned an invisible shield** <u>on my entire house and landscape.</u> Shortly after, I noticed my neighbor's sods were affected, while mine remained green. Eventually, the cold weather took it's toll on my grass. Nevertheless, there was a stark contrast in appearance, from mine's and the adjacent lawns.

Another time, **I utilized the invisibility cloak in my garden.** One evening, I applied the shield over my body. The mosquito bites were not as intense, as the previous day, without the shield. Hence, I can confidently say, what had occurred was not imagined or made up. By the way, I did not used any pest repellents. This evidence has continuously reinforced my faith in God. Believing in him, has validated these events to be authentic.

The divine Lord is a spell-binding and powerful source, when the preponderance of unexplained miracles and justifications can happen. **An invisible shield is adept in masking and defending me against the dark diabolical harmful entities, or from any negative influences.** I alone, can safeguard my significant others as well.

INVISIBLE SHIELD

With this breakthrough, **I unpretentiously invoked God, to assist me in placing a double invisible shield, over entire Florida.** To protect the shores from the BP gulf coast oil disaster, and the hurricane season. I made a plea with utmost sincerity, not for personal self-gain, but rather human kind. Without God, this quest cannot be fulfilled, it must be a genuine united and collaborative effort. I am merely a vessel and humble servant for eternity, to create goodness in the world. With this heart-felt compassion, I feel compelled to serve humanity.

There are a myriad of applications. Utilizing defensive shield, to guard oneself from harmful UVA and UVB (the ultraviolet) sun's rays, and much more. However, I continue to stringently apply daily sunscreen, as a preventive measure. After all, I remain a mortal human being, not immune to the other elements on this planet. Such a powerful mechanism, cannot be lightly misconstrued, deft conscientious considerations, and future consequences must be addressed.

In essence, by virtue of devotion, I have to consistently remind myself of the cause and effect nature. For readers to comprehend and shed light into my philosophical thinking, **there is a dynamic inclusive reasoning within a reasoning.** To extend my sixth sense of wisdom, I probe into my inner soul for further instructions, validations, plan of actions or approvals, for final execution. As a reminder, wisdom and soul are all-knowing Universal truth, and acquired skills.

Throughout the perceptive, deep realm soul-searching process, I can pity those evil contemptuous beings, with buried hatred and bitterness in their hearts. With every encounter of the obnoxious and corrupted minds, I am only strengthened and reinforced with the power of emptiness. Forgiveness helps to propel one, to a higher phase of wisdom attainment and achievement.

SPEED PASS TO HEAVEN/ENLIGHTENMENT

A) Maintain A Pure Heart

This is honestly **the most burdensome to achieve.** Attainable, not improbable.
A good hearted person needs three basic foundations to build on.

First, perform continuous good acts. Actions speak louder than words. If your heart is not connected to the deed, it becomes null and void, thereby ineffective. Deeds are based on selfless acts, absence of compensation, or gratitude from the recipient. It encompasses an unhindered willingness to perform the actual deed, without the slightest hesitation, or deliberation. Furthermore, doing random acts of kindness for total strangers, out of one's comfort zone, is a gesture of receiving God's blessing, and favorable karmic returns. I cannot contain my high state of euphoria or adrenalin rush, after completing a good deed.

Second, saying good words. I have a habit of saying: "Wish you well." When you wish others well, in actuality, you are expressing bountiful benefits for yourself. It all reflects back to you. One needs to especially refrain from worthless gossip. Simply a nonsensical (nonsense) unbeneficial behavior. Spreading negative groundless rumor- not only harmful to one's soul, the words usually gets back to the intended victim.

I advocate speaking with caution. Erroneous statements can never be retrieved. **Misused information adds burden to oneself and others.** Creating a pattern of bickering back and forth. There is a sound reasoning to this concept. One cannot preserve the soul, while continually polluting it's wholeness. Being honest and truthful while using words, helps to bring forth integrity into one's being.

For Catholics, the "Ten Commandments states": "Thou shall not lie," is a foreboding wake-up call, to all who disobeys God's rules. **A monk once said:** "The least emotional burden contained within one's soul, the being dies in peace and harmony. Those with a lifetime of substantial burdens, ends in misery and suffering." This clarifies **those who fear death,** are usually wrought with guilt. Their conscience forbids them from dying in serenity.

I have witnessed this first hand, as a nurse. A portion of patients sleep comfortably in their beds at night. The same consistent ones, lie in their systematic chaotic episodes, of non-closure. Calling and shouting out a random person's name, climbing out of bed, for no apparent reason. Their souls ripped apart, catapulted from bygone actions of ill-fated deeds. There is a common cliché: "The past always catches up with you," certainly holds true.

Thirdly, the pathway for faithfulness- think Godly thoughts about others. This pertains to those who have mistreated, disrespected, insulted, prejudiced, made fun of you, either intentionally or by accidental means. No one states the passage to heaven was easy. A lengthy multiple, arduous-enduring journey, indeed. I am even at my wit's end, when being discriminated.

2) SPEED PASS TO HEAVEN/ENLIGHTENMENT

A) Maintain A Pure Heart

Incidentally, I have to once again keenly retain in mind, I am a unique resolute (faithful) being, and reflect upon nothingness. More often, the misfortunates are envious or resentful of those with wealth, better living standards, etc. Truthfully, when I was little, I used to pity myself from a poor childhood, and lack of a father figure. As an adjunct to awakening, **having propensity of gladness for others, is an insightful conditioning for spiritual correctitude (being correct).**

Comparing oneself to others, leads to discontentment and unhappiness in life. This persuaded me to focus on adverse society instead (homeless, poor, disabled, poverty stricken).

When a negative mental impulse arrives, I automatically say: **"Cancel negative thought."**

This **has a two-fold purpose: 1)** Lighten the burden within my heart, **2)** Delete the destructive processes of thinking/habitual cycle of irrational cognition (perception). These patterns leads to relentless unrest. Ultimately, blocking the nature of clarity towards compassion.

Formulating positive intention, includes avoiding spitefulness. Resultingly, the intended target is possibly ourselves. When mistreated, gather the inner strength of the moral side, to restrain thyself from straying into the diabolical path of hatred, or malice. Everyone has acquired a duality (good/bad) within themselves, in mitigating reaction, and the decision-making process of action. **The dwelling darkness, is a consistent force to lead us astray.** Towards greater conflicts of spontaneous malicious ill-will, in an attempt to retaliate. These devastating powerful emotions will take over reasoning, sabotaging all the other senses, and knocking them out of synchrony (arrangement). Plus, the convenient repetitive mental blame-game strategy, is a potent excuse to relinquish our own responsibilities, as a human being. This should be realized during our moments of angst, or outburst against the other individual.

Finally, in order to conform on a course of consistent favorable wishes, **shun hateful influences and organizations** catering to demeaning others. Either by gender, race, or sexuality.
Associate with those who have well-grounded intentions in life (good, kind spirits).

B) Avoid Addictions Of Any Kind

The **second easy-pass towards heaven-** not inheriting any forms of addictions, during your life cycle. Addictions includes: Drugs, smoking, alcohol, compulsive gambling, criminal acts, or lustful sex. Each dependency sets you back a lifetime.

The journey cannot resume, unless the poison is purged and cleansed. The previous life cycle with such contaminants, continues repeatedly for an unspecified time, to be totally rid of it's impurity. The cause determines the effect, of how many lifetimes to be duplicated. Until one gains final success, for the actual path towards salvation and deliverance.

Time and again, humans commit the identical repetitious sinful acts, lacking self-recognition of the root cause- themselves. This becomes a blinding non-existing oblivion to nowhere. Essentially entering a dreary tunnel, without guidance of light, within the darkness of no return.

Do you apprehend **why it's burdensome to convert poor behaviors?** They consists of past and present memories, which deters or prohibits our progress for change. After living through half a lifetime, I now comprehend the causative (cause) factor, responsible for the individual's stubborn resistance, in motivating the necessary alteration of one's actions.

Memories are monolithic (massive) emotions, adhering to the heart and core of our dilemmas. Creating reminders, either desirable or disturbing, to affect one's journey. Inevitable past experiences, have a direct impact of inciting phobias into one's life. Adding burden, and hindering progression of the life cycle.

The ever-present **disadvantage of recalling detrimental memories-** one becomes entangle with a constant build-up of guilty conscience tendencies. This is not healthy, per se. The prevailing intellect develops layers upon layers to protect it's fragile ego, insulating against further insult.

Perhaps this explains individuals who possess dual personality traits, or schizophrenia. Their state of mind has become ill-equipped in dealing with the multitude of daily stressful activities.

The psyche (mind) compensates by splitting into multiple personalities. Merely to emphasize, the mind is vulnerable. There exists a breaking point, when all coping mechanisms have been exhausted. Draw a mental strategy. Devise a plan to activate in motion. Liking and loving oneself, is the first initiative. Avoid destructive mental behaviors (the self-badgering of negative, anti-productive thoughts). **Locate the source of the problem.** Confront them without fear or hesitation. Seek advice when in doubt. Perseverance is the key.

The easiest method, in avoiding any form of abuse, is through prevention. One cannot ascertain balance or harmony, by harming oneself with toxic substances, a lethal cocktail of disastrous results. So futile, allowing external factors to dictate a pandemonium of unpredictable consequences. **Assuming self-control, is the quintessential approach in mastering the game of existence.**

C) <u>Return To A State Of Pureness</u>

Of all enduring tests, **this is the most demanding to achieve.** Once accomplished, it becomes a powerful asset to guard oneself against the Satanic forces. We are confronted with critical decisions. Thus, the benign choices paves the fate, in deciding our karma. **The pendulum of coincidences, are intersecting and intertwining with precise accurate intention, and purposeful motives, to challenge us in every direction.**

The direct passage to heaven or enlightenment, is returning to a condition of wholeness/pureness of heart, mind, and soul. Easy enough to grasp. Evidently immensely exhausting. However, attainable eventually. Occasionally, we have encounter the bombardments of unexplained circumstances that surprises us out of nowhere, rattling our nerves with unpredictability. To combat this, I seek guidance from God, in the form of a prayer. The almighty Father is attentive, if you open your heart, and allow him into your life. This requires commitment and strong faith, to validate the process. The Lord says: "Ask and you shall receive."

Maintaining a state of pureness, requires a lifetime's devotion. Initially, the heart must not be tempted with spite, whenever an individual is insulted or ridiculed. The soul's original state is pristine, void of hatred whatsoever. One needs to sustain an equilibrium of love, compassion, forgiveness, kindness, good deeds, and integrity. For all fellow human beings. The darkness is eager for us to fail.

Concentrate on the positive aspects- apply it to your advantage, to surpass into a state of purity. In my personal life, I have been trampled by **racism** many times over. During each of those episodes, **I have forgiven them.** I return to my state of pureness, which is love. **Forgiveness** is a therapeutic spiritual healing tool, to remove the burdens placed by others. Difficult to initiate, yet immensely liberating.

The continual **integral path towards pureness-** necessitates a daily self-conscious reminder of consequences, regarding our actions. This practical approach succeeds in affecting the reasoning, or rational part of our consciousness, to remain disciplined, with the incentive of good behavior.

Another defense against the dark forces, is tolerance. A Chinese proverb: "One day of patience, equals one hundred days of fortune." **The ritual of endurance-** is a training tool to withstand sudden adverse situations, aimed at throwing us off-course. Maintaining a calm behavior, induces logical thoughts and deriving plausible problem-solving dexterities. In a sense, avoiding immeasurable sufferings.

The realm (kingdom) of life, is an unrelenting influx of stress, problems (external and internal), unexplained forces, that invades and disrupts our sense of order, and sanity. Instead of reacting to these problematic occurrences, I have reached a resolution. I retreat to my solace of solitude, reflect and ponder what has transpired. Within the quietude of my soul, I obtain counsel from my wisdom.

C) Return To A State Of Pureness

A tranquil mind, permits me to examine the critical significance of the circumstance, towards self-spiritual revelation. The answers provides valid basis for clarifications, and inducing my bond with God. He is the reason for my existence. Through God, is the manifold (many kinds) source of expansive knowledge, and spiritual truth. **Solitude enables me to evaluate the multitude of variables,** affecting my diverse in-depth decision making abilities. To delve into one's wisdom, is listening to the heart. An assessment of pro or con alternatives, are then judged in light of deep faith principles. In achieving spiritual awareness and enhancement of holy attributes, contributing to good deeds, actions, and intentions.

Seeking a religious purpose in life, sets forth the foundation to pave the way to pureness. The antidote to cleansing your heart of contaminants (sins), is connecting with God, or whatever faith you attribute to. Once the spiritual entity embarks onto the soul, it allows the person to instill a journey of self-purification, and further wisdom advancement.

One stage is profound clarity (the fluidity of clear thoughts comes easily), the ability to observe relevant, false facades (others take for granted), and deciphering the righteous course to proceed. The holy spirit provides a safety net, guarding us against every conceivable event, projecting our way.

We have often heard of incidents, where an individual has survived a deadly plane crash, while everyone else have perished in the aftermath. This is divine intervention. There is an appropriate phrase: "Know God and you shall receive salvation."

D) <u>Continuous Conscious Amendments</u>

There are a plethora of inconspicuous poisons, attributed to our own self-doings. Most common are daily communication functions via: Social networking (e-mailing, texting, tweeting, skyping) and speech (wrong words, lies). Unbeknownst to the sender (if the communications are not sincere), with the addition of false pretenses and broken promises, these ripple-effects mounts to a lifetime of sins, towards the end of one's cycle.

The antidote is elimination of amassed toxic procurements, to minimize the burden. One must seize the opportunity, promptly rectify the offense, and make amends. **Removing crumbs on one's slate** (avoid buildup), is an efficient spiritual device to cleanse the soul.

The decisive power, is possessing the least cumulative dust pollutants in our souls. By virtue, you have enter a monorail speed-pass, surpassing the supposedly determined life cycle. An admittance to an advancing phase, of the clock-work precursory (something to follow) course. In effect, **skipping from one point in time to another, in the space-time continuum (boundless).**

****

****

FORMULA FOR EXIT STRATEGY

****

ZERO TRAPPINGS = **ADVANCEMENT**
(INTACT SOUL) **(TO SPIRITUAL SPEED-PASS)**

TONS OF TRAPPINGS = **DEFERMENT**
(CONTAMINATED SOUL) **(BACKWARDS CYCLE)**

****

****

A Quote From Thornton Wilder:
"Those Presumptuous Souls Who Wanted To
Walk On The Pavements Of Heaven."

E) Think Of Nothingness

How did I derive nothingness? Through a lifetime of enduring devotional faith, and spiritual awakening. I finally attain the true meaning of life. In the summer of 2010, I was in a Buddhist temple, contemplating. Suddenly, my wisdom said: "Think of nothingness." From that moment on, the concept of my existence transformed. This has confirm my reason for living, I was intended for a higher purpose. **What is nothingness?**

The paramount focus of nothingness- **simply reflect on emptiness. Nothingness is a directional compass, to guide mind/spirit/body into a reflective mode of tranquility,** without being affected by any trivial interference that heads our way. There is no extreme happiness or sadness. Being calm and content in the moment.

Receiving a verbal insult without any reaction or altercation, is a true testament to the supreme intuition of exemplary understanding. There is no physical pain being inflicted. When the condition warrants no reaction, it becomes nonexistent.

Emptiness is conducive to centering one's path.
Towards advancing spiritual reasoning on (4) levels:

1) Harnessing astute, insightful spiritual resources.
2) To be in a compassionate state of mind.
3) To ward off spiteful behaviors.

4) To banish negative thoughts from appearing or inciting any emotions to act out the deed.

With each succession of benevolent feats derive in one's lifetime (a mainstay of pureness: Heart, mind, spirit), the journey to God's holy kingdom is elevated at a quicker pace. Be mindful, to distant yourself from the quick sands of sinister allures. While encountering temptations of failure, ask God for guidance. Prevail in your heart with determination, and dedication to eradicate any evil notions presiding within. **Think of the white light.** The wise adage: **"Karma follows every act."**

Achieving nothingness is not a small measure in itself. Mainly the purest of hearts can acquire distinct fluid knowledge, reserved for uncontaminated souls. The space-time earned virtues, determines one's spiritual status. Comprise with each passage of life, comes greater advancing tasks to test one's abilities. Retain the holy spirit within, inspire thyself to fulfill the destiny.

Absolute total honesty within oneself, is a decisive precursor (forerunner) for retrieval of emptiness. Truth in reality (for awakened beings), is a powerful invisible cloak in defense against the besiege of insidious wicked burdens. When untruthful to thyself, it becomes a mirror-image of deception reflecting back to the individual. Forbidding him or her from garnering clarity, and seeking power from wisdom. "Say what you mean, and mean what you say," is my motto.

Another essential ingredient- the ability to embrace solitude for lengthy periods of time. Easier said than done. Humans are social creatures, yearning to be loved, and accepted into the social network of society.

Why is solitude so important? This is a blessing in disguise for the faithful, dedicated to God or True Source. Serene silence is a blissful spiritual state of being, in focusing magnanimous devotional discipline. A conceptual basis for fathomable soul-healing respite (rest), and gravitational (gravitate) mode/access to underlying thinking hypotheses (verification). **Within the realm and fortress of seclusion, precious wisdom can be obtained within the time frame of, a milli-second in time.** The power of true knowledge is inside us. Consider the similarity of the priest's or monk's daily meditation rituals, alone in remote locations.

The inner thoughts of reflective, contemplative reasoning, becomes more readily available, lacking any distractions, in the confines of quiet solitude. The sound of silence has a reservoir of insights, ready to be retrieved in episodes of deep spiritual awakening. There are creative ways of reaping these resources, by means of meditation, or with tranquil thought-provoking self-inducements (a compassionate state of mind, preparing benevolent deeds).

Isolation provides a safety quarantine against negative influences. An evil entity has the power to implant dark seeds into the subliminal subconscious mind. We become exhausted or feel deprived. Suddenly the energy in us, is completely depleted of strength and stamina. Concentrate on serenity, which is impervious to turmoil. **Imagine an impeccable luminescence, with the heavenly Angels embodying your spirit. Be in peace with thyself.**

From my wisdom point of view, emptiness is comprehending the law of the Universe, an absolute righteous entity. This is a valuable knowledge, safeguarding lure of the dark Lord's (devil) temptation to assert wrongful harm.

Actualizing (realizing) the true meaning of nothingness and applying it, are two separate issues. One must instinctively apply the indispensable powers, during unforeseen and unprepared circumstances. This realistic portrayal, is a testament to self-awareness and realization of grasping the concept.

E) Think Of Nothingness

On August 2010, I perceived another self-revelation in acquiring nothingness, at a milli-second instant moment. **Emptiness is obtained** when mind, spirit, and soul are in complete unison and perfect alignment, at a particular elliptical space (two fixed points are the same constant) in time. Actually by accident. There is no intentional purpose involved. In a natural, and balanced state. In my case, the culmination of years in isolation, has finally succeeded in fulfilling this knowledge. The interplay of long-term conscious humility and self-sacrificing deeds, were domineering factors in reaching this phase.

This exam is exceedingly arduous to succeed, my faith and trust in God was constantly challenged by self-criticism, and insecurities. I was not loved by family, society, no one for that matter. I felt all alone in this world, aside from my husband.

****One accepts the immediate proximity of time for it's worth, without reaction. The hours and minutes passes by us in life, absent of pause or stagnation. Justifiably, I need to regard the passage of time, as is. Acknowledge the present in harmony and stillness, effortlessly with the beat of my heart and breath. Lacking any emotion, to glide cohesively as clouds in the sky, in every-day existence.**

This is my premise to disbelievers. I have confidence a Higher Source above, has been instrumental in determining my fate. There were immeasurable instances, where **I have been spared, in detrimental situations** (an attempted kidnapping on me, as a child, accidental aspirin overdose- when I was six, due to parental neglect). Being faithful to God, has direct consequences in having a good life at the present, and into the future.

****

******

****

*** ***I Like To Include A Humorous/Harmonious Gesture To The Readers. In The Movie, Kung Fu Panda: "There Is No Secret Ingredient."***

****

******

F) STRATEGIES FOR YOUR LIFE

We live in a world full of misdirecting signals. In one direction, are influenced family values. The other is what society dictates and expects from us.

1) **Define Your Purpose**

Searching a reason for living is not sufficient, one must seek his or her individual precise meaning. Devise an intervention, delineate a mental concept, what you desire out of life. Start from there.

2) **Choose An Appropriate Career**

We all need to maintain our existence with an occupation, in this world. The most vital criteria is to be happy. Pursue a positive, satisfying experience. Otherwise, it is pointless and futile to persist on this planet. Choose wisely, and cautiously.

3) **Follow The Righteous Path**

A majority of people fail in this category. They become intertwine with the lure of prosperity, power, and prestige. This is the most crucial process, it dictates everything else.

Be determined in present life. Follow a path of planting prosperous seeds for future endeavors. The very thoughts and actions we undertake, will determine the sequence of events that seal our fate.

4) **Do Continuous Good Deeds**

One way to increase or build spiritual wisdom from within, is through selfless random acts of kindness. Genuine intentions are techniques for procuring the framework of:

1. Intuitive reasoning.
2. Ethical principle development.
3. Awakening the senses.

There is a real connection with the soul, when an authentic gesture is extended from the kindness of the heart. This speak volumes, in solidifying the heart-spirit connection to awaken the wisdom.

When we replicate the Lord's unselfish acts of benevolence, in essence, we are receiving his blessings in reciprocation. The Higher Source is predominantly love and compassion. The act in itself, is a reward for the soul.

5) **Be Grateful/ Content**

Count daily blessings. Being healthy and alive is a miracle by itself, which we all take for granted. Mesmerize the present, absorb thyself with bright positive energy. Forget the problems. Breathe and exhale, as if today was your last day on earth.

Sharing My Deep Thoughts On Wisdom

*** First and foremost, I like to thank God and my wisdom profoundly (my guiding light). For the collaboration (our divine unison) of this book. I am eternally grateful.

*** To be reiterated: Wisdom is not easily attainable, you must have a good heart.

*** Wisdom can transform one's vision towards infinite clarity. An absolute sense of profound awakening. Which perpetuates the innermost level of the soul to a higher state, beyond space-time continuum.

*** Your soul is a camera- which monitors and records your every moment and motion (thoughts and deeds) till eternity. All those masquerades you have perpetrated- lies, deceits, facades, plots, and ploys are capture within thy soul. The reality: "You are only deceiving yourself."

*** Contrary to our beliefs or what we were taught. We chose our own journeys, prior to this life on earth. There are no coincidences. Each elemental incursion thrown into our paths, was a test. To determine and assess endurance, sustenance, of one's soul. The more arduous the task, the more successful you will become.

*** Recite: "Mind over matter," mantras to embed strength into consciousness.

*** Wisdom is not granted merely by individual requests. All determined by God, to bestow what you have earned. Dependent upon individual deeds and morals.

*** With wisdom, I retrieve information from my past and foresee certain events pertaining to the future. My wisdom had informed me, I was English and Italian in previous lives.

*** To me, I am no better than the sanitation workers, who picks up my trash every week. For we are all equal. <u>As long as you have two eyes and a nose, I am fine.</u> I respect all races. Gays, lesbians, transgender, different shapes and sizes. The soul is the thread that binds each and every one of us.

*** Seeking sense of purpose- requires strenuous amounts of introspective analysis, to derive and reach that zone and level.

*** Life presents obstacles in our paths. To incite the duality of good and evil, which resides in all of us.

*** The soul is the essence of our being. Do not take it for granted.

*** Throughout centuries and history, consequential life are pitted between good and evil forces. God and Satan have been duelling since the beginning of time. In the intermix, are human beings. We are merely experiments on this planet, like rats in a maze.

*** Conviction of the heart and concentration of mind- can overrule and dissuade any suave enticements, no matter how appealing it is.

*** No matter what your present station in life (physician, surgeon, attorney, etc.). It perishes entirely, once the cycle is complete. The remaining receptive wisdom powers one has attain, carries onto the next journey, and beyond. Immortal. Priceless!!!

*** Instilling good seeds into the heart- transforms the will to remain on the holy path of salvation. Creating and assuring luck, harmony, fortune, health, into one's direction.

*** The scope and magnitude of reasoning: The actual source is through the inner depths of one's soul.

*** Art, videos, movies imitate life. They inundate our lives with false delusions and for escape. Distinguish fallacy and reality. After the mirage, re-insert realistic mindful attributes worthy to your daily living.

*** Again, thank you God. For the insight of nothingness, the opportunity to serve you, to have love, compassion, and understanding towards others. From the bottom of my humble heart!

CHAPTER TEN

CULTIVATING A PHOTOGRAPHIC MEMORY

The King and I: "Getting to know you."

Having a photographic memory, is **an essential and irrefutable tool** in our daily existence. Not everyone has this ability. Imagine, having an agile mental flexibility, to re-examine the source of what was lost, and being able to retrieve it in a matter of minutes. **This application is beneficial to the** real estate industry, business, tactical analysis, forensic applications, scientific functions, architectural detailing, and every day settings. We all have misplaced things in our daily lives-trivial as car keys or miscellaneous items. The noteworthy documents: Birth certificates or passports, that are crucial to our identity.

As I mentioned previously, I never had a mentor to educate me. I inherited the capability in early childhood. **This fortuitous technique was self-taught.** I grew up in a laundry. The assorting of clothes and assigning accurate numerical numbers, were a constant redundant, monotonous task. I could not afford to misplace a garment, fearing my mother would punish me. A strategy I utilized, **was creating a visual imagery (image)** in my mind, or surrounding environment. I can efficiently back-track my own steps (self-rewind of prior activities) to locate the source. This auspicious gift has saved me. The immeasurable countless headaches, during the nine-plus relocations in our marriage. (Oh, what a migraine that was!!).

By reason, not everyone is equipped with photographic recollection. **It can be mastered and learned.** With anything in life, one needs to perform the exercises, and be patient. **It does work.** For beginners, designate a peaceful/tranquil environment to cultivate the discipline.

First, empty your mind of any annoying stress, or extrasensory stimuli. Retain clear lucid thoughts. Next, choose a harmonious room (favorite space in the house), void of irritating music and noise. Place two objects on a surface, focus/visualize it. **Concentrate with dexterity of mind.** Close your eyes, form a mental image of those two items in your mind. Again, pay attention. This **requires only a few minutes to perform.** Gradually, visualize other objects in the room. Or situate other materialistic details to the existing ones. Practice with your eyes, closed again. Then, without cheating, enter another room. Revisualize those same items in your mental thought. If you cannot recall specifics, return to the initial space, to assert a mental photograph. Repetitions are essential for perfection.

Do not expect instantaneous results on initial attempts. These skills are similar to driving a vehicle. The more you drive, the better you become. Later, when you are familiar and comfortable with the results, apply these exercises to the work environment. I prefer beginners to practice at home, since they are familiar with their surroundings. When you become more adept with your photographic memory skills, even a small item, such as a nail or thumb tack can be found. Subsequently, remembering or recalling can be achieved without any difficulty.

In photographic memory, I can reminisce with eye-piercing detail, insignificant specifics, even from my previous homes. I'm able to revisit the smallest attention of every painting, furniture arrangement, to the china in my kitchen cabinets. Anywhere I desire. **This asset is valuable. Allowing a person to research possessions, from ten to twenty years ago.**

Once proficient with unequivocal photographic aptitude, **the option to regain vital clues of information, is readily accessible.** Occasionally, it is unnecessary to shut my eyes, to ascertain the source. Unless exceedingly difficult, I merely darken my vision, and scrutinize for the object in my mind. There are instances, where my first attempts could be misleading. Nonetheless, eventually I succeed.

Suffice to say, the human consciousness is a powerful ally and arsenal at one's disposal, when seizing the opportune time to use it. Perhaps I had my wisdom in the beginning. Which explains, the succinct photographic skills came naturally to me. To the best of my knowledge, no one in my immediate family can accomplish this.

I would like **to share a specific example.** Without question, this indispensable tool functions. Having deftly advanced to another stage, I can retrieve items, that my husband never informed me, where he had placed them. One time, he exhausted an entire hour, searching for a re-certified medical certificate. I decided to help this poor soul. I walked into his study, and glance at the shelf. In a matter of two minutes, I discover the document for him.

In addition, photographic remembrance **has the quality to expand the mind into other different horizons.** I can recite precise selected memories from my past, with greater accessibility. I believe memories are blueprints of coping mechanisms. They are resourceful learning formats of assessments, from the past into future applications, or potentials. There is a saying: "History repeats itself." This is the rationale of humans, repeatedly committing their devious misdeeds. Despite being the most intelligent race on this planet, mankind continues to lack the fundamental principles of quality "humanness." Be wise, not solely through the intellectual side, but on the spiritual path as well.

Another significant aspect of photographic reminiscence- **using this resource to unleash subconscious pain.** How? By recalling or tracing past childhood experiences, various, or early beginnings. Refer back to the source which ails you, including phobias. For example, I contemplate on my childhood, where I had a repetitive nightmare. There was a constant dark shadow chasing me, unrelentlessly. I later realized, that reflection was my own mother. I had to overcome my fear of her. The photographic meaning can effectively pinpoint the point of origin, of the subliminal causes of suffering, and guide in rationalization and alleviation of the problem. **Unmask the cloak and hidden signs, underneath the visage (appearance).**

Once emotional healing has resumed, an improved person emerges. Focus on what is relevant. Build enduring relationships, and delete the extraneous burdens within thyself. Furthermore, we cannot assist others, unless we cure ourselves first. This process is **apperception. Which means acquiring perception, with full awareness.**

It is important for everyone to revitalize themselves, physically and spiritually. No one can do it for you. We must all gain individual responsibility, in maintaining a healthy lifestyle (proper nutrition, adequate sleep, regular exercise). Developing positive traits (integrity, virtue, good/healthy habits, self-reform), even if our parents lack morals. **Having a sound mind, and body is life-sustaining to one's well-being.**

Another approach concurrent with photographic ability- **facilitating logical reasoning in solving individual issues.** After accessing inception (origin) of the problem, ascertain answers. Inquire the source in thyself, to purge forth the correct responses. We are complicated beings, with intricate labyrinths (passages) dwelling deep in our minds. Attempt to derive the solutions.

****

****

INSIGHT OF RESILIENCE

****

RESERVE THE MENTAL STAMINA

AND STRENGTH FROM THE INNER

PLEXUS OF YOUR BEING. WILL-

POWER AND PERSISTENCE, DEFIES

TEST OF TIME ENDURANCES. IGNITE

THE FLAME AND EMANATION OF

GOODNESS, TO EMBODY THY SOUL.

TREASURE THIS, TILL THE END, OR

LAST DYING BREATH.

MAE LOUIS

****

****

CHAPTER ELEVEN

THIS BEAUTIFUL WORLD

Avatar: "I see you." "I see you."

Out in the spatial (space) galaxy, mankind has always been mesmerized by the gamut and magnitude of it's wonders. With each succeeding space exploration phase, the gathering of information is intriguing, and baffling to the human spirit.

Using this framework of thinking, I would like to expand this subject matter further. The human soul is constantly curious, in a never ending quest to source the knowledge. In part, to enlighten themselves into the far reaching atmospheric realm of the unknown.

Despite these efforts, **mankind still has a decade of learning to acquire.** The points of origin are right under our noses. Aztec Civilization, Stone Henge in England, the Lost City of Atlantis, to name a few.

The secret of spiritual shadows: Is an inescapable phenomena, with immense sublime and supreme powers beneath. Encapsulated intricately in devise (arrange) form, undetected to the naked eye. Corresponding to the galactic (galaxy) stars, the earthly entity (our planet) spontaneously dispenses eminent consequences and so call non-specific, untimely occurrences (earthquakes, tsunamis, whirlwind tornados). To awaken our senses, for incoming unprecedented predicaments.

Sadly, our civilization has come to a standpoint: Calamity and war between nations, terrorism, unspeakable acts of violence amongst humans, hate crimes, the lists goes. The human race should be ashame of themselves. Rightfully indeed. Advance of science, medicine, technology, and decoding the latest complex cryptic cell structure, contradicts exactly what we are capable of manifesting. A null and void endeavor.

Unlocking the mystery is attainable. To reach the unreachable stars, we must first master the basics. Our ancestors before us, have delineated a path with their demonstrative executional plans. **To survive, unity was the clue.**

The human species can progress as an entire continuum, in total unison. Without the barriers of race, color, or prejudice. By collaborative means of educating one another as a planet, in a united forum, not in competition form. Rather, gaining aspects from each other, in awe of our individual strengths and weaknesses. **Unification as a world, is the key to opening the door: To a beautiful, exulting, peaceful realm we all deserve.**

****

****

****Live In The Present Moment, Aspire Goodness/ Kindness To All Fellow Men, Women, And Children Kind On This Earth. This Is My Evoking Message.***

****

****

And yes, from achieving supreme wisdom, the embodiment of incredible awakening is source-able in mid-air. Effortlessly, with the blink of an eye. A total mind, body, heavenly connection, exceeding the dimensional speed of light. Far greater than searching for the stars or landing on the moon.

The underlying subconscious **(spiritual) instructional manuscripts,** from our previous civilizations, have foretold and projected a pathway. To direct, and lead future generations with this foreboding wisdom: "Their determination and will to survive, came as a realistic conclusion. To remain united as a whole, or plunder into ruins."

******

****

AN IMPORTANT ANALYSIS

****

Sight unseen, sounds unheard, are the epiphany attunement of surpass awakening. In the epic silent episode, stands me. I am alone. Equanimity (serenity & composure) with the Universe in everlasting peace. Next to his divine presence- God. Non-sequential (unimportant) self-reasoning of all inconsequential (insignificant) matters, fades into the sand. My formidable calmness is in direct reflection to the ocean, earth, and every ounce of living composition on this planet.

Entering this passage of time, there is no movement. The translucency of my soul evades permanently into the transparent light of infinite, unspeakable wholeness. This is a description of: Holy aperture (opening) / fortification (strength) of wisdom, spirit, combine into one.

****

******

FATE:

What is fate? Fate is the supposed force, principle, or power that predetermines events. Fate has a derived purpose.

I am amazed, stifled at the inexplicable occurrences. The coined phrase: "No coincidences," expresses this clearly. My intense self-contemplation, has enable me to decipher this wisdom thinking.

For unspecified circumstances one wishes to avoid, **fate interjects and intervenes with split-second accuracy to determine one's self.** Closure or completeness is an unending circling device, to measure the depths of the individual's soul. Specifically **the passage of time:** Past, present, and future were decidedly placed, and set up as events in our paths. This is called the "conditioning phase," (exhibiting or trained to exhibit a conditioned response) of human life. Each of us are experimental forces in the realm of existence.

In this matrix, (situation) the rare and few distinguish souls who acknowledges this awakening, can apply instantaneous resources, to reach to another phenomenal transformational level of time and space.

To explain this in layman terms. With penetrating spiritual insight, not only can I envision my frontal third wisdom eye (located between the eyebrows), behind as well (becoming all-knowing). In terms of time, age is of no concern to me. For I am aware of anti-aging secrets, within my reach. This I will covet to my grave. Space is relatively of no consequence. I navigate through time and space-travel, with my soul to definite destinations at will.

SELF-INTROSPECTIVE HUMAN ANALYSIS

The enigma (or obscure riddle) of life, is a spellbound phenomena in itself. Within it's point of axis (unlimited line), is the relationship between human soul, and the galaxial (galaxy) entities that exists reciprocally in our lifetimes. So complex, the intricacies manifest quantum leaps of past life journeys, crossing towards present and future episodes.

The prophecies (predictions) into the future, are from the past. **These stationary microscopic minute spheres of pre-memory existence, lies beneath our spiritual subconscious-cortex (outer layer) zones.** By utilizing the capacity of harvesting (or salvaging) existent underlying experiences (from all past lives), one can alter the aspects of spiritual destination to supreme heights.

In a way, by telescoping (visualizing) into total accumulated lifetimes, unfolds a compiling of innumerable exponential data embedded in those spiritual vaults. Circumstantial episodes (events) becomes reality. **How did I attain this paramount knowledge? In a nano-second in time.** Acquiring these celestial meanings **(from the prodigious holy kingdom's spiritual literary world)** is a testament, to my human will and self-probing tenacity, of deep spiritual awakening aptitudes.

I LOVE YOU WORLD!

****

****

*** ***<u>MY WISDOM TO ALL:</u>***

"WHAT MATTERS IS INSIGNIFICANT, NOTHINGNESS EXISTS."

****

*** ***<u>BEHOLD:</u>***

"HEAVEN AND EARTH ARE LISTENING."

****

****

QUESTIONS & ANSWERS

1) How can I become a human lie detector?

It involves three instrumental components. First, be true to thyself (entirely honest). **Second,** being truthful to all fellow beings. **Third,** trust only yourself. This encompasses no assistance from anyone. All while maintaining a clear decisive spiritual heart.

These are crucial stages, in the development of forming self-knowledge. In achieving the foundation to become receptive, this requires life-long purpose, and commitment. Humans habitually deceive themselves and others, without any sense of guilt or remorse. Essentially, inflicting self-damage to thy soul. Certainly the incorrect path to pursue.

Frequently, the individual has actually provided the hidden answers. To discover the truth, dissect their sentences and words to interpret it's significance. An example: "I'm going to send you the money." In the real sense, the person is establishing a delay tactic. A reality seeker myself, I can easily discern their true representations, into the actual essence of the message. **When utilizing astute hearing skills,** explore inner speech intonation (sound) and depth. **In sight,** indirect eye contact or shifting of the gaze, conveys deception and evasiveness (masking the true signal). The other indicators, are body language, deeds, and actions.

Why did I succumb to my own downfall, in trusting my mother? Love is the instigating factor in all emotional matters, in blocking our senses. Which coins the phrase: "Love is blind." Most importantly, I did not trust myself. Unknowingly at the time, I've became the weaker link. I allow someone to dominate me.

In conclusion, the answers you wish to inquire, are already present with their words. Why do we regret bygone remarks? Reason being, it can never be retrieved. Statements are irreversible, and permanent. Simply, the existing proof and evidence is right in front of you. <u>In order to search for light in the tunnel, one cannot be blind himself or herself.</u>

2) What can I do to protect myself against the dark (evil) side?

The devil comes in many forms, to entice each and everyone of us (a seductive temptress, insatiable greed, etc). Make no mistake, the clever dark Lord is cognizant (aware) of all foibles (weaknesses) within the innermost realm of our being. The least deviant behavior one has, the less prone he or she will fall into Satan's devious traps.

We should adhere to the Ten Commandments, or our individual religious beliefs. These laws have **an intentional three-fold purpose:**

1. <u>Preserve/protect one's soul from further damage.</u>
2. <u>Keeping us grounded, towards the light.</u>
3. <u>Achieving individual salvation.</u>

There is a simple analogy: To maintain life in perspective. **Visualize thyself as a fish in the ocean. A bait is on the line, to lure you in. If one is able to remain below the radar, avoid each temptation, the greater success in defending against evil.**

QUESTIONS AND ANSWERS

3) Can you see a person's soul without looking into his eyes?

Personally, I prefer to see the individual initially. To obtain an accurate reading. By way of photographs, is also an effective means to peer into their core. An exception to the rule: I can detect via the phone from voice resonance (vocal tone) and word, to gain some perspective. In fact, **a remarkable moment happened** two years ago (2010). I was conversing over the phone with my landscaper. After he completed the sentence, I instinctively visualize him (in my mind) picking up a pen to record my remark. The following time, I inquire him in person, to validate my curiosity. His answer was: "Yes, but it was a blue pen." Without a shadow of a doubt, I am able to view his actions from far away distances. I am amaze of how accurate this ability can be.

Sadly, **supreme wisdom is a double-edge sword.** I can succinctly sense a person's heart-felt feelings. Most frequently, the honest truth hurts. In every intuitive meaning of the word, these overwhelming experiences, further strengthens my resolve to remain, and maintain on the holy path.

****

******

****

I Have Finally Realize The Segway To:

<u>**ASTUTE WISDOM COLLECTION**</u>

****

<u>They Consist Of:</u>

1. ***Attaining The: Twelve Levels Of Consciousness.***
2. ***Pre, Present, Future Life Acknowledgments.***
3. ***Acute Sixth Sense Awareness.***
4. ***Phenomenal Wisdom-Eye Alertness.***

****

******

LATEST UPDATES

1) As you all know, **I had previously implemented an invisible shield for my husband's mother.** She is currently ninety-five years old. In June 2012, she fell in front of her son, on concrete flooring. Again, no fractures or injuries were sustained, only bruises. A compelling testimonial indeed. This shield will protect her for life, which were my original intentions. The credit goes to God, not me.

2) A few years ago, out of extensive self soul-searching and reckoning. I finally accepted the fact **my mother will never, ever love me.** I am nothing to her. With this shock-wave inner sensation, I could have become bitter and remorseful. Instead, with absolute committed virtue, I reached for the valuable source: Love. One day, in an instantaneous moment, with tears unrelentlessly flowing down my face, **I begged and implored to God: "God, I have no love from my mother. Please end my life right now, and give it to her!! That is all I have left to provide her. I am willingly asking you to do this God!! I don't care about my life!"**

Remember, I said there are no coincidences. With the earth-shattering thunder and lightening request, **I was diagnosed with ovarian cancer** in September 2011 (strikes one in a thousand). No, almighty Father did not end my life, as I had wished for. As an alternative, this is as close as it gets. The tremendous post-operative surgical pains were at times, like living hell (a knife into the wound). That is a justifiable description, of the enormous torture I had endured. I became a ninety-three pound skeleton. Nevertheless, if my mother's life was extended for an extra ten years, it was well worth the effort. No regrets on my part.

I have not seen my mother for fifteen years. After my full recovery, I visited her and relayed this story. I verbally forgave her. We have finally reconciled. What is most important- heaven, earth, and sky must have focused on me that day. **Love for my mother is profound, beyond time and destiny. I will always love you Mom.**

AFTER THOUGHT

To my beautiful readers and souls. We all exist on this planet for a reason. The air we breathe is a testament of that purpose.

I poured my heart and soul into this book. With far-reaching source from all-knowing wisdom, to share with others. This was twenty years in the mental planning stages of development. It has been a life-long quest and resounding search, culminating completion of this book, and bring about successful fruition of my destiny. I hope the profuse message will inspire everyone to find their definition, spark intellectual and spiritual growth within themselves. What did this journey teach me? "I will never stop learning, till the day I die."

Our souls were meant to aspire to the heavenly mountains and sky, in recognition of our true selves. To behold and accept the absolute validity of our individual being, in acknowledgment of it's pure essence.

To everyone, I wish you all a peaceful journey ahead. May your wisdom shine it's bright light, and lead you to the final destination.

Here is what I would like you to consider. In this book, I have provided you solutions. Wait. There is more to it. Within the elaborate contents, lies a hidden labyrinth (passage) of answers upon answers, if you can locate them. Your mission is to derive your individual responses. Sorry, no free rides. Goodbye.

P.S.: THANK YOU FOR READING MY BOOK, FROM THE BOTTOM OF MY HEART.

****

****

****

*WISHING YOU ALL LOVE, HOPE,

AND PEACE. TAKE CARE EVERYONE.*

ACKNOWLEDGMENTS

HONORABLE MENTIONS:

To God: "Without you, I am nothing."

To my loyal and devoted soul mate/ husband: Sin P. Lee, M.D., F.A.A.F.P.

Mom: "I will always love you, till the end of time."

To my special brother: Howard Louis, D.P.M.
"I love you Howard, with all my heart."

Venerable Chueh Fan
Director of Guang Ming Temple (Orlando, Florida)
Thank you for the emotional support during my greatest moments of upheaval- cancer.

John V. Kiluk, M.D.
Sachin M. Apte, M.D.
Moffitt Cancer Center (Tampa, Florida)
With sincere gratitude for your utmost professionalism, and adept skills as a physician.

St. Peter & Paul Elementary School (Brooklyn, New York)
Former Fr. Bob Cevasco, Sr. Jamesetta (4th Grade),
Ms. Martinez (6th Grade).

P.S.: I Am Truly Grateful To Have Met
Each And Everyone Of You.
I Wish You All: "A Good Life."

Mae Louis was born in Brooklyn, New York. She earned a B.S. degree in nursing from New York University. She currently resides in Tampa, Florida. The author has dedicated her life in the search for the real essence and meaning of life, to lead others in their quest for spiritual awareness and awakening, empower those lost souls toward inner embodiment of wisdom, knowledge, and insight.